Leading with the Brain

Sebastian Purps-Pardigol is a leadership coach and organisational advisor based in Hanover, Germany. Renowned neurobiologist Professor Gerald Hüther encouraged him to combine the insights of brain research with management training methods. Together they founded the non-profit project ›The Culture Change Code‹ (www.the-culture-change-code.com).

Sebastian Purps-Pardigol

Leading with the Brain

The 7 Neurobiological Factors to Boost Employee Satisfaction
and Business Results

Foreword by Gerald Hüther

Translated from German by Romana Love

Campus Verlag
Frankfurt/New York

The original edition was published in 2015 by Campus Verlag with the title *Führen mit Hirn. Mitarbeiter begeistern und Unternehmenserfolg steigern.* All rights reserved.

ISBN 978-3-593-50668-5 (Print)
ISBN 978-3-593-43562-6 Ebook (PDF)
ISBN 978-3-593-43563-3 Ebook (EPUB)

Editors: Tonya Blust and Daniel Wilson
Cover design: total italic, Thierry Wijnberg, Amsterdam/Berlin
Cover illustration: Think stock
Typesetting: Fotosatz L. Huhn, Linsengericht
Printed in the United States of America

www.campus.de

For
Paul & Harry

Contents

Foreword by Gerald Hüther

It has now spread: In the course of their lives, everyone has acquired specific skills, collected certain experiences, and acquired specific knowledge in certain fields. All that makes a person who he is. But during his or her life, he or she still has the possibility to learn something new, to acquire new knowledge and new skills, and to make new experiences. So it's possible throughout a lifetime to evolve and to grow beyond oneself. This potential is created in the internal organization of the brain from the outset. No one can fully develop all of his potential, but everyone has, no matter how old he or she is, the possibility to use this potential to acquire new knowledge and to acquire new skills. Nobody can force him, but only invite, encourage, and inspire him.

However, many leaders have a problem with this, not only at school, during training, or at the university, but also in businesses and organisations. That is why so much of what students, apprentices, or employees know, and therefore can apply, stays far below the possibilities. The teachers in the schools, the instructors in the companies, and the professors at the universities can live with this. The continued existence of their institutions is not jeopardised. However, businesses and companies work differently. They cannot survive in the market, and they can go bankrupt if their employees do not want to evolve. It is no longer sufficient if, every now and then, someone will tackle issues, think along, and take responsibility. Companies today, especially in our culture, need employees who want to get involved and for whom it is a pleasure to explore what else could be improved.

In principle, companies and organisations do not work much differently than a brain. They also have a potential that is greater than expressed in their balance sheets. In principle, a lot more can be achieved, however, not by applying more pressure or even better control. With these measures, short-term successes can be reached. In the long term, this strategy undermines the commitment and willingness of the staff to develop their potential they possess within. As a result, they will only do what they need to and what they are paid for, and that's not enough for the long-term success of a company.

So the question is whether and how it could be better. It is this question I have been exploring with Sebastian Purps-Pardigol for several years. Not in theory, but in practice. We have been looking specifically for companies that, somehow, managed to do it, in which leaders successfully invited their employees, encouraged and inspired them to unfold the scale of their potential. Where employees have found their pleasure for thinking independently, rediscovered their joy for joint creation, and cheerfully participated in a much different way, growing beyond themselves.

We both had experienced how hard it was to describe the important elements of implementing new findings in lectures and workshops. All these theoretical considerations don't gain sufficient persuasive power, until they can be made verifiable, tangible, and comprehensible through practical examples. That's why we have been searching for such practical examples of successful cultural change processes in organisations and companies for several years. We did not want to use the organisations advised by us as case studies to avoid a subjective coloration and distortion. So we had to be attentive and to find companies that appeared to be appropriate to us. Sebastian Purps-Pardigol has spent a lot of time with the companies in question to talk to business leaders, managers, and employees. On the homepage, www.the-culture-change-code.com, we presented a selection of practical examples, and I am happy and grateful that Sebastian has put together the findings and insights of recent years and provided them to our dear readers in this book. In this book, he describes the mystery of how such a change of previous management and relationship culture in companies and organisations can succeed.

Even though the chosen ways and strategies might be different in each company, it becomes clear everywhere that one thing is especially important: Employees feel they are no longer used as objects of ratings, arrangements, measures, or the interests of their executives. They want to be seen as subjects, who are trusted. There are no special methods or techniques used in these companies by the executives. It is rather a different, special mind-set that allows these executives in different ways to invite, encourage, and inspire their employees to develop their own potential. This is where the secret of success can be found: You cannot do it, you first must find out by trial and error how to do it, how to do it better than before, and that it primarily depends on the improvement of relationships between all parties. Wherever a relationship culture is based on appreciation and care of each other, where all employees of a company pull together and pursue a common goal, the economic success will sooner or later result from this collaborative effort.

System theorists call it »Self-optimisation of living systems.« They are currently trying to understand the phenomenon underlying this general principle: In every living system, the involved subsystems (in a business these are the employees) organise their relationships in such a way that the required energy expenditure for the preservation of the relevant system is as low as possible.

However, in many companies, this principle becomes evident in its negative expression: Because the relationships between managers and their employees, and often among the entire workforce, are so problematic, a lot of energy is used in these companies to compensate for these friction losses that result from these disturbed relationships to some extent. This may work for some time; however, such a relationship culture is not sustainable.

For several years, economists have been searching for new strategies that bring back momentum to the economic development. Their search is directed to the identification of the next innovation base to bring the desired upswing. By this, they mean pioneering inventions that determine the main direction of economic development for decades. The Russian economist Nikolai Kondratieff discovered the long waves that such innovations have on the global economy. Since the late eighteenth century, he was able to prove 5 such cycles supported by innovation bases, so-called Kondratieff cycles. The first cycle began with constructing the steam engine, the second with the production of steel and the invention of the railway. Developing electrical engineering and chemistry initiated the third; the fourth was borne by the invention of the automobile and petrochemicals. In the 50s of the last century came the driving force for the fifth cycle from Information Technology. Since then, economic growth was determined by the increase in the information sector. This cycle ended with the global recession at the beginning of this millennium.

Since then, the economic policy makers have been looking for the next innovation base. Meanwhile, they have identified the health sector. The sixth Kondratieff cycle will now be supported by improved productivity in dealing with health and illness. This area now sees a lot of vigorous investment in medical technology, molecular biology, wellness, and everything investors perceive as being relevant for health.

Perhaps, more health, more comfort, and increased productivity cannot be obtained through more diagnostics, medical technology, fitness equipment, and health clinics. Maybe to help people stay healthy, feel good, learn for a lifetime, and stay productive, something is needed that cannot be achieved with such policies and procedures. For example, employees in companies do not lose their pleasure in their own thinking and the joint creation. In this case, it would not be sufficient to introduce new technologies. Instead, the co-existence of people must be designed in such a way that everyone is invited, encouraged, and feels inspired to develop his talents and gifts, and thus his potential.

Then the basic foundation of innovation that determines our lives and our economic development in the next decades would not be a new discovery or invention, but one of particular attitude, a different self-image, and a different way of dealing with each other and with our nature.

Then growth would be made possible by avoiding the many friction losses. Then we could grow infinitely, without becoming larger and consuming more, just like our brain shows us: by improving and strengthening relationships between all parties.

I wish, dear readers, that Sebastian Purps-Pardigol can invite, encourage, and inspire you with this book to become more conscious of your own change-journey. The awareness we have already – we just need to apply it.

Göttingen, September 2015
Gerald Hüther

A symbiosis of science and economy

»The time is: 3 minutes and …« – the thunderous applause of over 3,000 spectators drowned out the rest of the words of the stadium announcer. It was May 6, 1954, a rainy day in Oxford. For the Englishman Roger Bannister, it was the most important moment of his life, because he was the first man in the world to run the mile in a time of less than four minutes. For decades, many athletes from all around the world had tried to break through this magic barrier. They had all failed.

But in the following years, something remarkable happened: Dozens of other runners finished below the four-minute mark. You might think they had adopted Bannister's training methods. But that was not the case, because Bannister had no special method. He was not even a professional athlete; instead, he was a prospective neurologist. The other athletes seemed to use Bannister's success as an »it-is-possible« example. They subsequently could rise above and fall below the four minutes.

»There have to be even more companies who have already succeeded!« In 2011, the neurobiologist Prof. Dr. Gerald Hüther and I discussed whether such a role model effect is also possible in the world of business at a joint hike with views of the Werra loop, a river near his home in Göttingen, Lower Saxony. We had already conveyed the knowledge of modern brain research – each of us in our own way – to many companies. And I advised and coached organisations in the long-term during a process of change, but now, Gerald Hüther and I were looking for a way in which we could start the cultural change by an effective impulse for many additional companies.

Entrepreneurs and decision-makers in many industries had already approached us with the urgent desire for change and development. In our discussions with many of these protagonists, we often experienced that they needed a little more than inspiration and knowledge. They understood well when we explained that connection is a deep-rooted, new, raw biological basic need, and every human being bears the desire for participation within them, or human action can be explained through the influence of inner pictures. A crucial piece of the puzzle was still missing: We needed »Roger Bannister« companies that could serve as role models for other companies and executives to give that last »It-is-possible« impulse. We needed companies that had already created a culture, based on people-oriented management. Companies whose workforce comes to work happily and enthusiastically, enabling stable economic growth. With such models, as Gerald Hüther and I knew, we could bring companies and leaders what they were longing for: such a culture to become reality in their own company.

The need in many companies to change something is evident and the economic pressure is not the only thing that has increased. The curve of absences related to mental health has been increasing steeply for years. Burnout and stress symptoms are now the leading causes of illness-related early retirements. The Hamburg-based corporation Unilever calculated in 2011 that the total costs accrued by mentally ill people add up to 7 million euro in the headquarters alone with its 1,100 employees.

The 1,500 corporate leaders interviewed for the IBM Global CEO study reported their companies were in such an economically complex phase that they rarely had matching strategies for the challenges lying ahead.

However, they believed – the CEOs responded in unison – they could overcome these difficult times better if they could use the creative potential of their employees. But how can they manage this if those miss work more frequently?

We didn't want to use the companies that were advised by us as »Roger Bannister« models. We thought that »one's own children are always the most beautiful ones. – We would not be objective.« Therefore, we started to look for other companies with lighthouse character that have employees who are measurably happier, healthier, and more loyal, thus are more successful than their competitors. It was a long search, but in the end, we found numerous examples. I spent a lot of time during the past four years studying the recipe for success of these companies in more detail.

In my role as an organisational consultant, executive coach, and author, I met the owners of organisations with 40 employees and CEOs of companies with a 50,000-man workforce: fruit juice producers, hotels, law enforcement agencies, fashion companies, chain stores, cosmetics companies, manufacturers of special machines, winter service providers, and many more. During my long conversations with bosses and employees, I was especially interested in these questions: What conditions had the decision makers of these companies created for their employees? With what inner attitude had they created these? Which different behaviours had they developed, so people in their companies could grow beyond themselves?

I experienced employees who cried when the manager left their companies, people who set up working groups in order to »preserve the good spirit« of the company in the long term, a student who suddenly received a hotel management position from the boss of a hotel group and achieved historically good results, a workforce that jointly developed a corporate strategy that resulted in a sales growth of 70 percent, a company that increased its sales from 1 billion to 1.6 billion after the employees had made it the focus of their attention.

Over the years, I was able to recognise recurring patterns in these companies. What I saw was the manifestation of the neuroscientific findings I had learned from Gerald Hüther and other researchers, whose humanistic attitude has influenced me sustainably. Science, I realised, provides pertinent explanations for economic success. I explain these patterns of success in this book for you. Let yourself be inspired!

Chapter 1

Big Bang – You are the person with whom change begins

> »If someone aspires to change within a company,
> he is well-advised to start changing himself first.«

Bodo Janssen, Managing Director, Upstalsboom hotel group

»Good morning! My name is Bodo Janssen, and I have this vision of happy people.« Two things are obvious about the Frisian man with his hands in his pockets. First, he is not wearing a dark pinstripe suit like most other speakers at this Economic Conference in Berlin. Second, he begins his lecture without rehearsed opening phrases, without a PowerPoint presentation, and without finely honed rhetoric. Bodo Janssen says what is close to his heart and in a way that hardly any listener can escape its spell. He talks of happy employees, collective retreats in monasteries, and the personality training he undergoes with his team. By the time Janssen almost casually mentions that sales in his hotel chain, Upstalsboom, doubled in just over three years and that guest recommendations increased by 98 percent, it is so quiet in the room you could hear a pin drop.

It's spring 2013, and Bodo Janssen is the last speaker before I take the stage. After I finish, we barely have time to exchange business cards. A few weeks later, we meet in the restaurant of his Berlin-based hotel. I want to understand how he got his hotel group to where it is today: One of the most desirable and profitable employers within the industry.

As in many other conversations I have had with leaders of companies that maintain successful corporate cultures, one thing quickly becomes apparent: Even here, the change within the company started with a personality change in Janssen. Surprisingly open, he told of devastating poll results among the chain's employees, of years filled with sleepless nights when his first company encountered economic issues during the establishment phase, and of life-threatening days when his family faced extortion. That changed him in a positive way.

Other executives attempted to guide their employees in a new direction, though usually at a greater personal distance. I had experienced a memorable instance in Berlin a few years earlier. After the neuroscientist Gerald Hüther and I had taken up joint work, word spread quickly: We wanted to uncover the secrets behind the achievements of successful corporate cultures. Institutions outside the field of the economy had heard about us. I was living in Zurich, when I received a call from a German Federal Ministry. At the annual Head of Department exam, they wished to hear what we had discovered about admirable corporate cultures in the previous years.

My visit to the Ministry should shape me significantly, albeit differently than I expected.

Two months later, I presented some of our experiences to the Berlin Ministry. After I had finished, the heads of the departments looked at me, puzzled. With sharpened pencils and a clean sheet of paper, they wanted to know: »How can we achieve a culture just like the one you described? What exactly should we do differently in our ministry?« Something about these questions irritated me. I felt like Jamie Oliver being asked for a spaghetti recipe. In my mind, I compared all the executives Gerald Hüther and I had talked to or advised: They were all people who had managed to achieve measurable and noticeable changes in their enterprises. Suddenly, I became aware of the difference. It was the inner involvement; it was enthusiasm. That's what was lacking in the faces of my listeners this morning. »Don't change anything in your ministry for now,« was my intuitive response. »The first sensible step would be to change something within yourself. As long as you, as an individual and a team, don't know where you want to go and why this is important, you should not even begin.«

The response to my advice in Berlin was rather retentive. A Secretary of State, who participated months later in one of my open trainings, was amused when I told her about it. »In these organisations, people are more used to obtaining concrete instructions for action rather than a recommendation for self-reflection,« she said. »The professional life shows that mostly reactive action prevails there, and the time for long-term considerations is not sufficient.«

The observation of such an obvious »non-involvement« of the executives was an important indication for me. It explained what I have seen so far in successful corporate cultures. Something I took for granted until now: All executives who successfully created a human and economically thriving culture started this process by working on themselves, first. It seemed as if there was a common unspoken understanding among these people. A long time ago, Mahatma Gandhi put it like this: »Be the change you want to see in the world.«

What do we want to tell our grandchildren?

Bodo Janssen's early years at Upstalsboom were difficult. Initially, with developing his own company, he wanted to step out of his father's »big shadow.« In 2005, he returned to the family business and later took over sole leadership of the Frisian hotel chain. The finances were solid, the customers were happy, and so was the staff. At least, that's what Bodo Janssen believed. But when he employed a new head of HR, Bernd Gaukler, in 2009, Bodo Janssen learned the following: »Mr. Janssen, I have the feeling I am working for two companies, here. One company is the one you describe. The other company is the one your people are describing to me.« Gaukler suggested an employee survey, saying, »However, I may be wrong.«

A few months later, a devastating result became apparent. »If our employees graded us back then, the results would have come back as poor to very poor,« says Janssen. »The statements were clear: The dissatisfaction among the employees had much to do with the leadership and the executives,« Gaukler reports. Accustomed to success, Janssen, as head of the company, was stunned. He retreated for a few days to the seclusion of a monastery to process the feedback of his chain's employees.

Bodo Janssen learned early in his life to let go. As a child of wealthy parents, he was the victim of a serious crime in 1998. At 24, as a student, he had been kidnapped. His captors demanded a ransom of millions. Again and again, they staged mock executions. His kidnappers put him on a chair, placed a bag over his head, trained a pistol at his neck, and released the trigger. Whether they were playing Russian roulette, or whether the gun was never loaded, Janssen doesn't know. »Successively, I let go of unimportant things in my life,« says Janssen. »At the beginning of this torment, I still entertained thoughts like, ›Now I won't make it to my next university lecture,‹ or, ›I just bought this nice, new car.‹ Every time they conducted one of these mock executions, I modified these ideas and reached a greater depth.« In what became for him, as he says, a »crucial and formative period,« he learned to distinguish the essential from the inessential. Since then, it has been easy for him to separate the former from the latter.

Many years later, in the monastery, this experience helped him with the realignment of his business. »What is essential?« This was his central question during the days he spent behind the sacred walls after hearing the devastating employee feedback.

While staying in the monastery, Janssen developed a personal mission statement. He also asked himself about which experiences in life touched him the most. Finally, he realised those were all moments when people were deeply happy and moved. »One day, when I am a grandfather, sitting with my two grandchildren on my lap before the fire, I do not want to tell them about great business results and operating margins,« says Janssen. »I would much rather like to talk about something that touches them. Something they may remember for a long time. I'd rather talk about how many joyful people there are in our organisation – because this is, unfortunately, not the case at the moment.« Therefore, Bodo Janssen decided, still in the monastery, to align the focus of his hotel chain to produce happy people!

With these thoughts, Janssen returned to his business. He incorporated his thoughts into the company's vision: The happiness of its employees became the corporate strategy.

»Initially, I did not believe him,« Bettina Cramer recalls. Cramer is Head of Administration for the holiday apartments at Upstalsboom and has been working in this field for a decade. Previous challenging experiences had taken their toll. »At my last employment, I had a catastrophic, choleric boss – not nice! And even at Upstalsboom, some things weren't all that good in the past. The employee opinion survey made that clear. I thought, ›Just because Bodo Janssen is a new boss and wants to do everything differently, I won't bring myself in immediately!‹«

That Bodo Janssen had gone to the monastery after the poor survey took many by surprise. »I thought at first, ›What kind of nonsense is that?‹« smiles Bettina Cramer. »However, when he returned, something had changed about him. That was the first time I thought, ›This guy does more than just talk. He indeed means what he says.‹ He understood what had gone wrong in the past. He recognised that he had to start with his own personality change.«

»At the beginning, I thought that all Mr Janssen wanted was to get our attention briefly,« remembers Anne Stickdorn, a banquet coordinator from one of the hotels in Varel near Oldenburg. »I would not have expected he was really serious about going down this path. For many years now, he has been implementing exactly what he says. Every one of us recognises that. That's why we trust him.«

Bodo Janssen focused on himself, first. »Initially, I set little behavioural goals and measured myself against whether I achieved them. Every day I worked on myself,« he remembers. »I spent a lot of time reflecting on my thoughts, my feelings, and my behaviour. Initially, I hoped to be calm and level-headed in all my decisions.«

Janssen's personal change was only the kick-off. He wanted to convey this experience to his employees, as well. »My time in the monastery was so formative it was important to share this experience,« says Janssen during one of our meetings in his Berlin hotel, while drinking green tea. The way he thanked the waitress at eye level, I could feel how important relationships are to him. »First, I invited all 70 executives to spend a few days in the monastery,« he says. »Sixty-eight of them followed my invitation.« In groups of 15 participants, the executives from North Germany started by spending two blocks of three days each in the Benedictine Monasteries in the South of the Republic. In the time to come, employees in non-leading positions could join, so they, too, could have this experience. »I was very happy when I was invited,« says lively sales representative Anna Heuer. »They were all talking so positively about the time in the monastery.«

»I was sceptical at first,« Bettina Cramer admits. »I belong to no religious group and, therefore, have no connection to a monastery. But after seeing the changes in our boss, I said to myself, ›Maybe there is something there for me, as well‹. As of now, I have been there three times.«

Inspired by his own time in the monastery, Bodo Janssen offered within the company curricula, which he leads himself. The curriculum includes three fixtures in which he works with a group of up to 18 of his employees on issues such as communication, personal values, or self-management. He leads up to five such groups each year. Those days are reminiscent of personality training, while at the same time increasing the connectedness among the participants, who equally represent the staff of various houses of the hotel group. »From the very beginning, I felt comfortable within the team and with all other participants,« says Ina Rogahn, Reservation Supervisor from the Berlin house. »Bodo Janssen managed to pick me up, so I wanted to get involved and develop personally.« Her colleague, Ursel Ortu from the Park-Hotel in Emden, adds, »The curriculum confirmed positively what I am doing and helped me to achieve my personal goals.«

Through his actions, Bodo Janssen not only gained the trust of his staff on his path towards »happy people,« but he also made his vision a reality. That perceived happiness increases when people get involved, he quickly understood. Rather than delegating from above, Janssen often integrates his employees into decision-making processes to give them an opportunity to participate. »In the past, a directive was given from above. Today, however, everyone is actively involved in all strategy development. That enables us to identify more with what we are doing,« says hotel director Jeanette Dedow from the Berlin house.

»I often experience a lot of appreciation from Bodo Janssen,« reports banquet coordinator Stickdorn. »Even though it sounds weird: We see him as one of us!«

»Frequently, he asks for our ideas on some issues. You can tell he subordinates himself and his opinion to the vision of happy people,« says sales manager Anna Heuer. »He gives me a free hand in many things.«

»If you let go, you have two hands free.« This is one of Janssen's favourite aphorisms. He repeated it in many of our joint meetings, and he acts accordingly. By now, Upstalsboom is almost fully led by staff, not by the head of the company. »They are doing a better job than I am, anyway,« smiles Janssen. He finds more fulfilment in helping the employees of Upstalsboom identify new ways in which they can continue to grow beyond themselves. Janssen realises not everyone is where he could be. »I assume that 25 percent of our employees do not even know what we are doing here. We create an environment in which every individual can develop optimally.«

A young woman, not even employed full time by the company, enjoyed the advantage, as well. Yvonne Klein had applied only for an internship. The student wrote her undergraduate thesis on Upstalsboom and wanted to get to know the company from the inside. Janssen, however, who had recently closed one hotel, made an unusual offer: »How would you feel about re-opening our hotel and running it as a summer internship?« After a week of consideration, the student accepted the proposal.

»You mean a hotel you just recently closed, you want her to re-open again? And you want it to be organised by a student, who has never worked for you?« I asked him.

»Yes, exactly,« Janssen gushes with genuine enthusiasm. The highlight is this hotel had the best income in its 30-year existence within the same year.

»Where did you get your staff?« I wanted to know.

»Mrs. Klein found them all. Five people for a 40-room hotel. However, she took out the catering part and remodelled it into a B&B. This way, she can run it with only five employees and some external service providers.«

During her study in tourism, Yvonne Klein repeatedly gained experience in the field of the reception of hotels. This was experience she needed before she could take over an entire hotel on an island at Upstalsboom. »You won't get such an offer very often,« she tells me on a foggy morning in Borkum. It is spring 2014. Her season hotel has just reopened after the winter break. »In the last weeks, I gathered experience at the headquarters and at Park Hotel in Emden.« Bodo Janssen has developed a mentoring system for Klein. The Emden house and its hotel director are now the main contact points for the young boss when she has to perform tasks for which she has not yet found solutions. »For a week, I was introduced to all the processes in Emden. In the meantime, hotel director Schweikard and I regularly spoke on the phone. However, the biggest challenge is the regulars, who constantly like to let me know that things are not the way they were for the last 30 years,« Yvonne Klein laughs.

»For someone with your family background, it seems easier for you than for most other people to strive for the best,« I tell Bodo Janssen in one of our last conversations. »After all, you grew up in a financially secure environment, and you never had to worry about existential questions.«

He nods and takes a deep breath. »Basically, I escaped from money. When my family had a lot, I was kidnapped. My life has been threatened. During those days, my capturers told me to choose which body part they would cut off, first. Years later, I invested all my savings in an ailing company, assuming I would have financial backup from my family. Shortly after, one part of the corporate group of my parents experienced financial difficulties. My mother had to pay the last personal reserves to the liquidator to keep her ability to act. My own business didn't do well either, and for three years, I simply did not know where to get the money to pay the bills. There was hardly a night where I could sleep.« Bodo Janssen pauses for a moment. »In an utterly threatening way, I have learned you cannot find contentment and happiness in money. Happiness is a matter of inner attitude. However, I only discovered that after this employee opinion survey had flown around my ears, and I started to look more closely at myself.«

Bodo Janssen shares his personal and daily experiences with his employees. With the same openness, he talks about difficult periods of his life and about success. »For many of us, Mr. Janssen has become a role model due to his attitude and behaviour,« says Anna Heuer. »He is the pioneer of our corporate values. When things get tough, we ask ourselves, ›What would Bodo probably do now?‹«

»I still remember some of my previous bosses, all from a hotel chain, as well,« says banquet coordinator Stickdorn. »When the car of one of the managers arrived, we all had cold sweat on our foreheads. If Bodo Janssen comes along, we are not only free from fear, we are pleased to see him! I know he wants the best for me and my colleagues.« Bettina Cramer adds: »For the 13 years I have been in business, this is the first time I feel that my boss sees and recognises me.«

But Bodo Janssen's leadership style doesn't mean a culture of mollycoddling. If needed, he can make tough decisions. After Janssen failed over two years to initiate a behavioural change in two particularly authoritarian executives, Janssen dismissed them unceremoniously. »The good of the whole is more important than the interests of the individual executive. And if I am forced to watch for too long how one individual shoots his poisoned arrows at a staff in his care and hurts the person, sometimes deeply, then I have to end this,« he said in a trembling voice. »However, professionally, I still respect them.«

Not only the guests, but also potential new employees feel the special atmosphere in the company. At a hotel opening in summer 2011, we had 3,000 applications for 100 advertised vacancies. This makes for 30 applicants per vacancy. The industry average is 0.8!«

»It is also surprising that the number of sick days has fallen rapidly since the economic aspect took the back seat and the human aspect moved to the forefront,« says head of HR, Bernd Gaukler. With a beaming face, Bodo Janssen adds: »In the hotel industry, employees work for an average of one and a half to two years. Our employees, however, stay an average of six years.« The better his employees feel, the better Janssen feels. And the figures show an investment in people's happiness is profitable for the enterprise. The turnover of the hotel chain Upstalsboom has doubled from 2009 until 2013.

> If you would like to learn more about Upstalsboom, look at this award-winning company-culture movie: leading-brain.com/upstalsboom

We can change an entire lifetime

Imagine I give you a headset to put on and let you hear a strange sequence of tones. Each sound is audible for only a fraction of a second, and most of these sounds appear to be the same. However, some are different. Imagine that, using a pen, I start to tap the back of your hand softly. Now and then, I change the rhythm. Now you have two stimuli: The sound from the headset and the regular touch of the pen.

Finally, imagine there is also a good friend with you in the room. He or she wears a similar headset and hears the same strange sounds, while the investigator taps him or her slightly on the back of his or her hand.

The difference between you and your friend is that I ask you to focus exclusively on the sounds from the headset and to give me a sign if you detect a change in the pitch. Your friend is instructed to provide an indication whenever the pattern of the tapping on his or her hand changes.

A similar experiment was carried out a few years ago with adult owl monkeys. They were trained to give a signal either upon a changing sound or a changing touch on their hand. The results led to pioneering knowledge in a new field of brain research: The so-called neuroplasticity. Neuroplasticity describes the brain's ability to change. Existing neural networks can strengthen, new connections between neurons can arise, and existing connections subside when they are not used any longer. »Use it or lose it,« neuroscientists call this phenomenon. For decades, neuroscientists believed this rewiring of the brain was possible only in children. Today, researchers knew they were wrong. Recent research shows the human brain can change throughout its entire lifetime!

For neuroscientists, that was an important insight turning an old belief on its head. In 1913, the Spanish Nobel Prize winner and neuroanatomist Santiago Ramón y Cajal had announced the adult brain is »rigid and immutable.« Although there were investigators whose studies reported differently, such findings in the world of neuroscience were not accepted and rarely published. In wise foresight, Ramón y Cajal added his words: »It is possible that the science of the future will show that this claim is false.«

In 1999, the time had come. In the prestigious journal *Nature*, the neurologist Daniel Lowenstein broke from the ancient belief: »For nearly a century, the claim of Santiago Ramón y Cajal was valid. It's time to put this dogma aside.« In his article, Lowenstein described numerous studies suggesting the adult brain is not only able to build new connections, but it can produce new neurons.

Many university neuroscientists began to examine intensely the phenomenon of neuroplasticity. Their findings provide plenty of encouraging evidence: Among London taxi drivers, they found a larger-than-average hippocampus – the part of the brain needed for orientation through the 25,000 London streets.

Researchers looked into the heads of averagely stressed managers at the Harvard Medical School and showed that, if the managers meditated a few minutes per day, their brains would significantly change after just eight weeks. They showed increased cross-linkages in areas of the brain responsible for learning, memory, and self-awareness.

Scientists also looked into the heads of professional musicians and realised, with the help of the latest technology, that they had developed different neural structures than non-music-playing people.

> **The realisation:** The old saying »A tree must be bent while it is young« is therefore disproved by modern brain research.

Unlike what has long been believed, the neurons in our brains are able to create new connections, strengthen those already established, or let go of those which are no longer used – until old age. From a biological point of view, at any time, we are able to change, acquire new knowledge and skills, develop new behaviours, and leave old ones behind. We can also adjust our way of thinking at any time.

Why don't we always succeed in this?

One answer could be obtained from events in the year 2004. The Dalai Lama invited several leading researchers from the field of neuroplasticity to his exile in Dharamsala, India. For several years, the spiritual leader of Tibet has met regularly with scholars from around the world to match the findings of modern science with the beliefs of Tibetan Buddhism. At the meeting in 2004, His Holiness and the researchers discussed the by-now-proven ability for people to change. The Dalai Lama liked this, because there was scientific proof of something Buddhists have believed all along: The human mind possesses tremendous potential for transformation.

The attending neuroscientist Helen Neville described the experiment with the owl monkeys, which were exposed to both the sounds and the touch – the way you were asked to imagine it just a few moments ago. With her report, Neville provided an important answer to how we gain access to our potential for transformation, how our brains become neuroplastic, and how we change.

Although, in the owl monkey experiment, all monkeys were exposed to the same stimuli, some were trained to pay attention to the sound, while others were trained to focus on the touch on their hands.

Once the researchers had conducted the experiment for a half hour every day for several weeks, they examined the monkeys' brains and had a ground-breaking insight: Those monkeys that had paid attention to the touch showed a significant enlargement of that portion of the cerebral cortex responsible for processing the touch of the hands. The area of the brain that processes the audio signals, however, remained unchanged.

»All those stimulations made no difference, because they weren't paying attention to it,« Neville told the Dalai Lama. »This is an beautiful experiment, because it shows the effect of attention on change.«

The researchers studied the monkeys of the second experimental group and found the two parts of the brain had developed in an exactly opposite manner. That portion of the cerebral cortex that processes the touch of the hands did not change. The part of the cortex that processes sound was restructured; during the experiment, the monkeys were paying attention exclusively to the sounds!

> The realisation: Attention decides whether someone unfolds his innate potential for transformation or whether he remains the man he has always been.

Attention opens the treasure chest of neuroplasticity. It decides whether something passes us by or leaves traces in our brains. This applies not only to stimuli, such as sounds and touch, but also regarding complex cognitive activities, such as learning new skills and, therefore, personal change.

Start with the internal pictures

After his stay in the monastery, Bodo Janssen could have returned to his everyday life and delegated the change in his business to its employees.

Perhaps, you have encountered this in your professional life: The boardroom announces a new direction and expects its employees to follow enthusiastically. During my time working at international companies, I often experienced this. In one entertainment company, many of us received a new motivational handbook. The president of our company read this book during his vacation and subsequently ordered it by the truckload. However, he had a unique interpretation of the content. He exchanged some executives and merged some departments unsuccessfully. The knowledge we gained from the book was of no interest to him.

In other companies, I experienced regular reorganisations about every twelve to eighteen months. If we were lucky, only the name of the department changed. In the case that we were not so lucky, we could throw the work of the past months – or even years – overboard.

Today, when a business leader asks me to escort him through a cultural change, I ask if I can talk with his employees, first. Only then can I can understand what makes the company tick. I often hear phrases like, »There was a lot of change in recent years. We are just tired of it.« Now is the time to tackle changes differently!

What helped Bodo Janssen and other executives, who successfully changed the cultures in their own companies, departments, or teams, was they gained a benevolent attention and a genuine interest in their employees! They didn't threaten the employees. That would have reduced the possibility of neuroplasticity due to an unfavourable mix of neurotransmitters. If you want to change the culture within a company sustainably, you need people who want and can change.

You can see a very entertaining movie about this research right here: leading-brain.com/carnegie

These are bosses who do not provide high financial incentives – because financial incentives reduce cognitive abilities, as researchers from Carnegie Mellon University proved a few years ago. These executives got to their employees with something else: They became role models who genuinely walked their talk, even in the face of numerous resistance.

Why is this role model function so important?

A brief experiment will show you the answer. Please imagine you are writing your signature on a piece of paper. Take your time. Pay attention in your mind to how the pen feels, what the colour of the ink looks like, and which sound the pen makes on the paper while you are writing. In your mind, write your name two or three times. Once you have done that, imagine you are writing your name with the same pen, but this time, you are using your other hand. Again, pay attention to how it feels, what you see, and which sound the pen makes on the paper. What is different this time?

Most people find it difficult to imagine writing their names with the other hand. If you can write with both hands, then imagine you are brushing your teeth with the other hand, or playing tennis or golf. The reason this is comparatively difficult is that the stable neural networks are missing. We perform certain movements only occasionally; therefore, the necessary synaptic connections in our brains are not as developed as those we use frequently.

There are only two ways to create these and other neural networks to initiate a new behaviour. First, people do something new. Second, they imagine it.

When the Dalai Lama first visited the laboratories of American neuroscientists, they wanted to impress him with a simple experiment. As with many visitors before, they had a student placed in one of their brain scanners; while he was in there, he moved a finger. On the connected monitor, the Dalai Lama could observe the activity of neurons in the motor cortex, which are responsible for finger movements. Most visitors were very impressed with this little show. The Dalai Lama, however, asked the student if he could imagine moving his finger, while his physical finger remained relaxed. The student complied with the request of His Holiness and moved his fingers only in his imagination. Just as in the previous experiment, the Dalai Lama could detect activity in the motor cortex of the student. The activity was slightly weaker, but the brain scanner proved that simply imagining a movement was enough to activate the corresponding neural network.

Numerous studies prove, through easily understandable results, that working with inner images can change our synaptic connections and, therefore, our behaviour. Through mental training, additional networks within the brain can be created. Thereby, people develop new responses or improve existing skills. If you give an unknown sheet of music to a musician and ask him to play this piece in his mind for an hour, he can play the piece of music after this time with fewer mistakes than his colleagues, who had the same piece of music, yet prepared it only on their instrument. If a basketball team takes time for mental training after physical training, their success rate will increase significantly.

The active, conscious process of imagination is one of several ways to change internal pictures and, accordingly, neuronal networks. Many top athletes, musicians, and actors use this method. If you have ever given a presentation to a large group of people, you have probably rehearsed your words in your mind several times before the event.

This process is suitable, even for people within a company, provided they have already decided on change and want to advance this development. Executives who successfully created a human-centred and economically thriving culture had previously developed strong internal pictures of the future state of their company – first for themselves and then with their colleagues and close associates. Often, those were clear visions of an open relationship culture, an environment of participation, more connectedness, work in a team, rather than a culture of roughs. The path develops through reflection and asking, »How would I like it?« followed by a joint discussion with the main protagonists.

The stronger and clearer these pictures are, the easier it will be to adapt one's own behaviour, and then to share this vision with the rest of the workforce. This unfolds a force that can be described as »incoherence«: Inner and outside worlds do not match any longer. This is the incoherence between the status quo of the outside world and the vision of the inner world. Because the brain prefers a coherent state, it will activate you repeatedly to change, so your external world matches your internal pictures.

The Nobel Prize in Literature winner George Bernard Shaw described this phenomenon – unscientifically, yet aptly – with these words: »The reasonable man adapts himself to his environment. The non-reasonable man adapts his environment to himself. Any progress is caused by the unreasonable man.«

Another way to change these internal pictures is to change the external pictures to which people are exposed. The things they see. The experiences they have. This is important for reaching your entire workforce and all those who are still undecided, cautious, and resistant.

In every company, some employees have had unfavourable experiences throughout their lives. They have already gone through one or more reorganisations, where they have lost something. They had supervisors who abused their trust.

Bettina Cramer, head of the department for the holiday-apartments at Upstalsboom, previously had a choleric boss. Because of this past experience, she came to the conclusion: »I do not trust my new boss.« She brushed off the benevolent assurances that Bodo Janssen just wanted to do things differently. She needed favourable external pictures to change her unfavourable internal pictures. These favourable external pictures developed as Bodo Janssen walked his talk. His consistent, long-term actions meant his staff developed trust. Banquet coordinator Stickdorn made this point: »Everybody noticed that he just does what he says.«

A brief reflection, and be honest with yourself. Assume you want to buy a new company. You have two employees, both of whom are knowledgeable about mergers and acquisitions. One of them has read a lot of literature about it, while the other has also coached three company takeovers. Whose advice do you trust more?

Another scenario: You need an urgent operation. Would you prefer to be treated by a senior doctor or the specialist, who has performed this surgery several dozen times?

Most people would trust those with more experience. It is the same with employees of companies: Just because you are an executive does not mean you get the immediate, unconditional trust of your workforce to facilitate cultural change in your company. On the contrary, some people may think you are not the right person for the job.

However, when you change yourself, you build – visible to all – experience-competence. If you develop a clear mental picture for yourself and subordinate your ego to the upcoming change, your actions will appear authentic to the outside world. Then you will receive something essential to the cultural shift: benevolent assurances and the genuine interest of your workforce.

In face of your future

During an event of the juice manufacturer, Eckes-Granini Germany, in February 2012, I experienced something unusual. CEO Heribert Gathof had just given his speech. Suddenly, two women went to the stage and took the microphone from his hand. Still out of breath, on behalf of the entire staff, they talked to their boss. »We want to thank you for everything done here from the boardroom, because that is anything but normal.« The rest of their 180 colleagues agreed with long, thunderous applause. Heribert Gathof, still on the stage, was embarrassed, struggling for appreciative words. I had been invited as a day lecturer and watched the scene unfold. Intrigued, I met with Gathof after that. It did not take long for me to detect that Eckes-Granini Germany was a company with a distinctive corporate culture. Its fluctuation was low, and it had happy and enthusiastic employees and a considerable economic growth curve (a doubling of the income within ten years). Those are just some characteristics of the juice manufacturer from Nieder-Olm. Even years later, Gathof remembers the situation back then. »The corporate event in February 2012 was one of the most moving moments for me,« he says. »The fact that my staff thanked me there on stage, I had not expected that, especially not in this way.«

Like many executives I met during my journey into exceptional businesses, Gathof is described by his staff as a »space-giving« and inspiring man, encouraging his employees to trust their own abilities. Chapter 3 describes how he developed the company's strategy through his employees and achieved sales growth of 70 percent. »With all that, which you receive in freedom and confidence, you just don't want to disappoint Heribert,« says the CFO of the company. In further discussions, many employees echoed this statement. Gathof has developed an attitude that undoubtedly touches his staff in a unique way. When, in January 2014, Gathof announced he would leave the company by the end of the year, because »he always thought, hitting 60, something new has to come,« tears flowed among employees.

Heribert Gathof's way started fourteen years earlier in the Swiss Mountains. For him, it was not a devastating employee survey, as it was for Bodo Janssen, but a slow, conscious process, which he started in the circle of some colleagues. »It was sometime in the 80s,« Gathof recalls. He was working in the marketing department of Procter & Gamble and handled the recently acquired product *WICK cough sweets*. Gathof and other executives were in the mountains for training. One particular exercise during this jointly spent time was loaded. The participants were asked to write their own funeral eulogies. »We were asked to imagine, who are the people who would come to our funeral – at some far time in the far future. What would people think about? Which of them would speak, and what would he say? Which of my characteristics would he highlight? Was there something those people better not mention?«

The funeral eulogy exercise is an effective method for people to become consciously aware of their own values and goals in life. »Some of my colleagues – particularly those who came from a different culture, or were at a different stage of life – ridiculed this exercise and could only do little with it. Others, however, just went with it. Even I felt a special affectedness,« Gathof recalls. »I had never asked myself questions about my funeral eulogy. I was fascinated by the things that not only happened to me, but to other colleagues. It was as if we entered a new destination in our navigation-system, or even realised for the first time ever that you could put in a destination.« What for Bodo Janssen was the conversation with his unborn grandchildren, for Heribert Gathof, it was his own funeral eulogy. The strategy, however, is the same. You look into the future, create new internal images, and adjust your life to match the new behaviour and goals.

For Gathof, an internal process had begun, which helped him reflect upon and understand many aspects of his own biography. »I was shocked by the funeral eulogy. Confused and shaken up. It contributed to [my] intensively look[ing] at myself,« he says. His life had been marked by ambivalent experiences. »During the difficult post-war period, my father had to take care of us. He was not the friendliest in the family. He could be very angry, even though a good-hearted man was inside him. Unfortunately, he died much too early. My mother always saw the good in him. It was for her I developed an attitude to always look for the good in other people.«

Perhaps, these early experiences are the reason for Gathof's »creative unrest,« which he repeatedly felt during his life. »However, until then, I never talked about it publicly. Nonetheless, those childhood experiences, growing up in a tense extended family, and processing those events were my driving force,« Heribert Gathof says thoughtfully. Still, years after the experience in the Swiss mountains, Gathof was impressed by the opportunity for personal change. Understanding himself better gave him access to his own potential. Most likely, much of his professional success had its roots there.

Gathof wanted to pass on his own experience. »In the '90s, my co-workers started to look at similar things,« he says. In his former role as brand-marketing manager at a company, he implemented a voluntary meeting each Friday night on the topic »Marketing between theory and practice.« In these meetings, he put questions to the attendees, such as: »If I had all the money in the world and did not need to work anymore, what would I be doing with my time?« Or »Who are the people I admire?« It was not uncommon for Gathof to share his own thoughts and answers with his employees.

»Many of my staff began to understand me better. I was tangible. Many of the usual insinuations, which employees often maintain against their superiors, didn't hold anymore.« Heribert Gathof changed his leadership style gradually, involved his employees more, and gave them more freedom for personal development. When he became CEO of Eckes-Granini Germany, he even handed the whole strategic development over to the workforce. »There are these famous areas of expertise with which you like to torture people. I believe you need to give your employees the right environment to develop. And then you must support them where they are already doing well.«

This approach has often paid for itself. For example, external consultants noted, at an SAP project, they rarely saw a team of experts with so much euphoria and passion for the cause. »I am proud of what we live at Eckes-Granini Germany,« says Gathof. »Repeatedly, I had business partners visit who told me that, while they had just asked to find their way around the premises, staff immediately told them the entire story of the company as well.«

In autumn 2014, Heribert Gathof handed the reins of Eckes-Granini Germany to his successor. At the beginning of this new stage in his life, I asked him what conditions he considered relevant for any executive to create this extraordinary culture. His response was consistent with what many other leaders to whom I spoke had told me. Two key points were essential to him.

First: »When I look back on my many years as a manager, I realise: The more attention I devoted to my own internal world and the more I got with myself, the easier it was to reach the people around me.«

Second: »I regularly delivered results. Otherwise, my superiors would not have allowed me to do what I thought meaningful.« That he knows his business, Gathof repeatedly demonstrated throughout his working life, first by a double-digit growth at Procter & Gamble and later by an even steeper turnover curve at Eckes-Granini. »When I started at Eckes-Granini, nobody there had heard about ›line-extensions.‹ So I implemented a brand design with the brand *hohes* C. Soon after, this brand had gone through the roof, and we created the basis for a long-term sales increase from 90 to 250 million litres,« Gathof grins. »While the market for fruit beverages was declining in Germany after the turn of the millennium, we created an opposite trend. We rushed ahead of the market by 50 index points. We just doubled our income.« During his time at Eckes-Granini, Gathof evolved from the marketing director of a division to the Managing Director of Eckes-Granini Germany. The business entity grew during his leadership to become the most successful of all 14 national companies. To date, it is the undisputed market leader in Germany.

Since Gerald Hüther and I have taken up our joint work, many people from the business community have tried to convince us their actions are equally newsworthy. Initially, we invested a lot of time into reading e-mails and documents or participating in long conversations. Over the years, however, a simple first filter has emerged: Only if an executive can regularly achieve satisfactory economic indicators will he be able, in the long term, to create a remarkable culture in his team, department, or company.

Heribert Gathof put it this way: »Our life was never ›dancing and singing,‹ but was marked by the shared will to develop our business potential.«

Essence for Executives

Big Bang – You are the person with whom change begins

- Successful leaders are a living example: Inducing change in your area of responsibility is best achieved if you change yourself, first.
- The hotel chain Upstalsboom doubled its turnover within three years, and employee satisfaction increased after CEO Bodo Janssen retreated to the monastery. There, he reflected on his own actions, aligned himself anew, and passed his findings on to his employees.

- Modern brain research proves that people, even at an advanced age, can change. The possibility of creating new networks in the brain and developing new skills is called neuroplasticity.
- A key competence that makes neuroplasticity possible is attention. Therefore, personal change among managers should be an attentive and conscious process.
- The attention of your employees – to make this neuroplastic change possible – cannot be forced, but only earned. Coercion and fear prevent neuroplasticity.
- You win the attention of your employees by being a role model. Heribert Gathof, former managing director of Eckes-Granini Germany, recalls, »The more time I have spent looking at my internal world, the easier it became to reach the people around me.«
- Keep the key economic indicators in mind! Culture change in the working environment must not mean running away from business challenges. Eckes-Granini Germany has developed one of the nation's outstanding corporate cultures and was, during this development phase, the most successful subsidiary of the Eckes-Granini group at the same time.

Chapter 2

Belonging – People want to feel connected

>Despite the obvious danger, apparently we all felt very safe.«

Olaf Glatzer, Director of Training and Qualification, Phoenix Contact

»The year 2009 was the worst in our more than 90-year business history. The global economic crisis took full hold of us. There were massive slumps in sales, and many employees were working part-time. We had to save tens of millions of euro in costs. I had some sleepless nights,« says Professor Dr. Gunther Olesch, managing director for HR, legal & IT of the family business Phoenix Contact.

In 2009, the Federal Republic of Germany experienced its most severe economic crash ever. Initiated by the financial crisis in 2007 and accompanied by dramatic events, such as the collapse of Lehman Brothers, economic output in Germany slumped by as much as 5 percent. In comparison, even in the oil crises of the 70s, the decline of the gross national product had never exceeded the one percent limit. The financial crisis affected the automotive industry especially hard. »The automotive markets took a downturn that had never occurred at this speed and intensity before,« warned the association of automotive manufacturers in late 2008. Phoenix Contact got its primary customers from this branch – the company specialises in Connective and Automation Technology.

It is a sunny late-summer afternoon in 2014. Gunther Olesch speaks quickly. Not rushed, but as if he would like to say ten other things at the same time. Every now and then, he jumps up, full of energy, because he wants to show something. At one point, he takes from the corner of his office a big picture frame with the corporate values and carries it to the boardroom table. You get the impression he feels passionate about what he speaks. There are no tactics, no retained messages.

The company for which he works has a turnover of 1.6 billion euro now – 600 million more than in 2009 – and employs 14,000 people worldwide. Headquarters: Blomberg. »Yes, we are not BMW in Munich – no big city, no known products. Nevertheless, we get a lot of applications – 800 per month. We can fill all vacancies!« says Gunther Olesch proudly.

Phoenix Contact | Years of crisis

In February 2009, the turnover is 14 percent below expectations. »What happened back then was new to me,« says controller Claudia Briese. »We had already had an economically difficult time in the past. However, as far as I can tell, it was regulated by the boardroom.« This time, the board of management called for a meeting with the entire workforce. There were company meetings for all Germany branches and a video transmission for employees abroad.

»I had to tell my employees: We had planned an 8 percent growth, and now, we are 6 percent below last year's sales,« recalls Gunther Olesch. »That is not good at all. We have to save 10 million euro. Imagine, you want to go for a four-week holiday and the washing machine breaks down. Perhaps now, you can go for only three weeks, because the money is missing. Please apply the same common sense to the company and see where we can save money.« Management indicated the sum and the entire team of employees was asked to look for savings. The difficulties should be solved jointly.

»This was a good sign for us,« Olaf Glatzer, director of training and qualification, recalls. »The truth is, we had felt for quite some time that something was not working right. It was comforting that the problems could be communicated so openly, without glossing them over.« However, the company had not yet hit rock bottom. In April 2009, the deficit of 6 percent increased to 15 percent, and by June, to a threatening 25 percent. By now, Phoenix Contact had to save 50 million euro.

In periods of high uncertainty, something happened that Jeanie Duck, a pioneer of change management, describes: »People connect the little information they get in the most pathological way. Executives must be very open and direct. They have to communicate more often.«

The management of Phoenix Contact did just that. Now, there were bi-monthly work meetings. The executives were visiting all local branches to reassure their employees: »We will do everything we can to keep you all employed.« Gunther Olesch recalls: »The security of the company and job security were equally important to us.«

Company: Phoenix Contact GmbH & Co. KG
Industry: Automation Technology
Headquarters: Blomberg, Eastern Westphalia, Germany
Established: 1923
Employees: 14,000
Website: www.phoenixcontact.com
Noteworthy: By focusing on its employees, the company increased its sales from 1 billion to 1.6 billion euro within five years.

The management made a decision: All non-executive employees went to part-time work, which meant less pay. Those employees had to waive 7.1 percent (of their former income). The executives were asked for the same reduction in their earnings. »The stairs must be swept from the top,« says Gunther Olesch. »We, from the management and all the other managers, had to waive the same 7.1 percent of our income.« This did not occur without any effect on the workforce. »Here, we are all treated the same,« was what the people to whom I spoke told me afterwards. Controller Briese said to me: »I cannot remember anyone who has complained. It was easier for us to accept the part-time work, because we were all in the same boat.«

And yet, in August, everything went further down. »I felt like a pilot trying to turn around the plane,« says Gunther Olesch. »You pull the controllers and nothing happens – because it takes a few miles until such an Airbus veers.« Meanwhile, the decrease reached a threatening 29 percent, and Phoenix Contact had to save 100 million euro. »Some things you never forget. The faces of our employees will remain in my memory forever. At company meetings, when we reported we were doing everything possible to create a turnaround, they applauded. But at the end, there were still frightened and sad faces.«

Olesch's colleagues contemplated redundancies, because if the decrease were to continue at the same pace, the company would soon be at 40 or even 50 percent below the previous year's sales. The executives concluded that up to 34 percent was possible; anything beyond would threaten the company existentially.

»How did you retain the belief that things could be done without redundancies back then?« I asked Gunther Olesch.

»I had and still have the conviction this company employs very special people, and together, it would be possible to reverse the current trend. I also had my moments of doubt, whether I was right in my belief. I also remembered former very difficult phases: Professional situations in which I had my doubts. Down in the dumps, where you think, ›That's it, there is no going on anymore!‹ And yet, there was. My life experience helped me keep my faith in the people and the company in the summer of 2009.« Gunther Olesch was right. By the end of 2009, the deficit had been reduced to 19 percent. Neither in 2009 nor in 2010 or 2011 did he have to let go of his employees. Actually, the cash flow was the best it had been in a long time: Instead of the predetermined 100 million, the workforce saved 120 million euro!

Repeated presence, jointly reduced salaries, and the authentic concept of »Together we will get through this« – that's how Phoenix Contact created stable conditions for its employees. »We older people could calm the younger,« says Olaf Glatzer. »If management says it cares, then it does. That's what I told my young employees. I have known the bosses for over 25 years: They keep their word!«

»This was the time when the two-year, external ›Top Job‹ employee opinion survey was due,« says Gunther Olesch. »Of course, we had our doubts if that was a good time. However, finally, we decided to go ahead with it, expecting unpleasant results. However, the result was surprising: In the worst year of our company's history, we were elected Germany's best employers.«

The crisis of 2009 was one of the most creative years of the enterprise. In these difficult times, many employees unfolded their creative potential. Many new products had been developed. Through their decisions and motivation, the executive level of the company provided security. In 2010, Phoenix Contact received the esteemed innovation reward, the »Hermes Award.« »Already, in January 2010, the switch was turned on,« says Gunter Olesch. »Customers bought many of our new products. Suddenly, we had a growth rate of 40 percent, and we switched from a three-day week to a seven-day week. With all the new inventions, we came ahead of all our competitors.«

Why everyone needs his monkey

What Phoenix Contact successfully demonstrated during the 2009 crisis is the fulfilment of an important basic need – one of the most critical needs we, as humans, bear within us: the need for belonging and connectedness. If this need remains unfulfilled, we feel bad. If this need is fulfilled, then this connectedness can stabilise us in the most difficult situations, because we maintain access to our innate abilities and potential. The high innovative ability of Phoenix Contact in 2009 demonstrates this in an impressive manner.

The need for belonging and connectedness arose early in us – in the bellies of our mothers. In these important nine months, we were connected around the clock. If we stretched our arms and legs, we touched someone. We felt the heartbeat and voice of our mother, and through the umbilical cord, we were always connected to her. After birth, we experienced a mother whose brain was flooded with the bonding hormone oxytocin. This bonding hormone ensures the mother cares for her child. Every time this feeling of being sheltered was missing, we did what babies do: We cried until someone came and attended to our needs.

It was a rather accidental discovery by pharmaceutical researchers that, in one of their experiments, they could establish the powerful effect of connectedness in threatening situations. They put a young monkey in a cage, with a growling dog hovering around it. The researchers could show the fear of the monkey in its breathing, its heartbeat, and the stress hormones in its blood. They got a second monkey and injected it with their test preparation: An agent intended to reduce anxiety and stress.

The second monkey was put into the same cage as the first monkey. As expected, the second monkey responded in a relaxed manner to the snarling dog. He showed no stress reactions. The researchers were satisfied: This worked.

But then, they made a surprising observation. The first monkey suddenly showed no stress response. However, as soon as the researchers removed the second monkey, the stress hormones of the first monkey flared up again.

The researchers repeated the experiment the following day, without drugs. Both monkeys were placed together in the cage, while outside, the ominous growling dog did its best to scare the monkeys. The animals in the cage remained without fear. The researchers concluded it was connectedness that made all the difference. They got curious and carried on with their experiments. However, the calming effect occurred only when they put a monkey from the same colony inside the cage – when the monkeys knew each other and had a certain connectedness.

Not until 2005 could a German-American research team explain why the stress of the two monkeys visibly lessened. Something fascinating happened: Whenever a monkey (and, by extension, a human being) feels connected to another, the hypothalamus – a four-gram part of our brain – secretes an important neurotransmitter, the same one that floods a mother's brain shortly after birth: the bonding hormone oxytocin. This has a calming effect on the amygdala, a central part of the fear system of the brain.

The realisation: Connectedness is a good sedative in moments of great uncertainty and fear.

Phoenix Contact | Like the phoenix from the ashes

»It took us 80 years to reach an annual turnover of 1 billion euro. Since we focused on the people in our company, we succeeded within five years to increase our turnover to 1.6 billion,« says Gunther Olesch. »In the painful crisis, we understood even more how important the people of Phoenix Contact are for economic success.«

»I think it was important for the management to realise we employees could handle open messages – even if they were negative,« remembers controller Claudia Briese. »It was like a spark that developed between us in the time to come: More connectedness.«

After the crisis was over, the employees wanted to continue with regular contact with the top bosses. »It was obvious the management could not see 14,000 people regularly, particularly if there are many locations,« Claudia Briese remembers. »That's how I came up with an idea back then: If it is not physically possible, perhaps it is virtually.«

Briese suggested the management make regular camera recordings for the entire workforce on daily issues and updates and strategic topics. Those short films should then be accessible to all employees as a »video podcast« on the intranet.

Owner Klaus Eisert and his management team liked the proposal. After a few weeks, the idea was implemented, and the first recording was done. »For employees, it was important to see equally as much of each of the five executives. Up to then, some of them had remained rather in the background. Those video broadcasts made them more present for us,« Briese remembered. »Soon after the start of the project, my colleagues from Production told me how much they liked to see a new podcast every two months. Before, they would see their executives only once or twice a year. Now, they can decide when they want to see the boss, because the video podcasts are available at any time.«

Initially, Claudia Briese led all the conversations. In the meantime, however, there are several employees running the interviews to whom the bosses must answer regularly. The interview questions range from the quarterly review of the current employee opinion survey to the development of various trades. »We show the latest movies in the weekly briefings of our production staff,« says production department manager Burkhard Wenzel. »This ensures every employee can actually see them. Following the short film, there is an opportunity to discuss what they have seen.«

For employees, the video podcasts are an important tool for immediately hearing and seeing the management's concerns, if not in a face-to-face situation, then at least digitally. But vice versa? What are the options for the management to understand better the concerns of the 14,000-employee company?

In many businesses, contact with the Board is possible only through the intermediate management. Naturally, each supervisor has his own filter. Consciously or unconsciously, some information is passed on to the upper levels within the company, and other information is not. Phoenix Contact circumvents these natural filtering mechanisms. The company has created special roles for 30 employees: the »trust-facilitators.« They selected employees, who already enjoyed great acceptance among the workforce. The management set out to be perceived by the public as the most trustworthy company in the sector by 2020, and thereby remain independent in the long term. »If we do not want to be merged with another company, then we have to grow. And we have to do better than our competitors,« explains HR development manager Martin Grosser.

»To be perceived as more trustworthy towards our customers, we first need a high degree of trust in our team.« This was the conclusion of the medium-sized company. That's where the trust facilitators come into play. From each department, only those who showed a long-standing, well-connected association to the employees were selected.

»Most of us are veterans,« says Olaf Glatzer. »Take me, for example; I have been with the company for 40 years.« The trust facilitators initially formed a cross-departmental network that met regularly and exchanged developments at Phoenix Contact. They are the first contact for their colleagues, consultants for the unit leaders, and middlemen for HR, and for management. This helped Phoenix Contact establish a back channel from the employees to the executive level.

»The trust colleagues watch closely how what comes from ›above‹ is received further down the hierarchy. They do not belong to the HR department; therefore, they are like a neutral seismograph,« HR Manager Yamilet Popp explains. »Through them, we in HR, and management as well, recognise even better when and where we need to do something.«

»In addition to the trust facilitators, is there another form of direct contact between the top management and the employees?« I wanted to know.

»I know a lot of companies with 400 employees in which the employees never get to see a manager,« says the head of the department for training and qualification, Olaf Glatzer. »We are 14,000 people, but whenever new trainees start with us on the first day, a representative of the management is in the room to tell them a bit about Phoenix Contact. That's quite fast.«

»As part of the trainee program, dialogue with management is always on the agenda,« adds Gunther Olesch.

To mark a fundamental strategic ten-year orientation in 2012/2013, owner Klaus Eisert and his colleagues travelled to all the company's sites for nine months to meet with a total of 1,200 employees. »We had developed the preliminary draft of a strategy and sought feedback from our employees,« says Olesch. Every week, from 9 am to 5 pm, five managing staff met with an at-least-20-member group to present and discuss the current strategy. Employees of the Human Resources Development moderated the workshop.

»As a participant, it was interesting to learn what concerns and thoughts the CEO has,« says head of the production department Wenzel. »That gave me lasting peace of mind in the company.«

Every Monday, beginning at 1 pm until night, the five CEOs met to discuss the feedback from the previous week and to work and refine their concepts. »Overall, we performed 89 of these workshops with staff, in which we discussed and developed the strategy,« says Gunther Olesch. »Previously, I worked as a business consultant for big enterprises and for a large steel company. I remember well how it was there: Every few years, the management came up with a new strategy. Then expensive business consultants were brought into the house and refined the concept. Finally, the expert handed the final policy papers over to the board. I know more than one company in which this approach went gravely south.«

»We are thus successful, because we pull at the same rope as one big team, and not just economically,« continues Gunther Olesch. »The people here are measurably healthier and loyal. We have a health status of 97 percent, as a manufacturing industry with a three-shift system. The national average is 93 percent. Our turnover rate is one-tenth the national average, and we don't even have sexy products. It must be due to something else.«

Loss of belonging | Worse than a prison sentence

In 1967, the psychiatrists Thomas Holmes and Richard Rahe presented a list of 43 events that can affect a person's life decisively. The list included items, such as a change in the working environment, pregnancy, or the taking out of a personal loan. Holmes and Rahe asked about 5,000 people to give each event a stress value from 1 to 100.

The survey was published under the name »Social Readjustment Rating Scale«. The top three high-stress events are: 1. Death of a spouse, 2. Divorce from a spouse, and 3. Separation from a spouse. These three events were ahead of job loss or a prison sentence.

Since the Social Readjustment Rating Scale was published in 1967, Western society has changed in many areas. Economic dependency in a relationship or marriage has become less important. Women are more financially self-determined, today. However, social exclusion and a loss of belonging remain among the biggest stressors people face. In 2002, Roy Baumeister, professor of social psychology at Florida State University, conducted several experiments. He proved that people, just through the thought of losing their connectedness, lose a significant proportion of their cognitive abilities.

In his experiments, Baumeister divided the participants into three groups. Each person was first subjected to an extensive personality test. Following the trials, the participants were given an evaluation from Baumeister's team. The first part of the assessment was given individually and corresponded to actual results, which should have raised the endeavour's credibility among and acceptance by the participants. The second part, however, was made up. Every participant in the first group received feedback, stating he had a personality structure that justified the conclusion that, for the rest of his life, he would build strong social ties and maintain lifelong friendships. The participants in the second group were told they had a personality structure that would lead them to face injuries and hospitalisation throughout their lifetimes. The participants in the third group were the actual test group. The fear of no longer belonging was stoked in those people. Researchers told them they would always lose friends, love relationships would break down, and they would have only a few friends, if any.

Following the constructed evaluations, the subjects of all groups participated in an intelligence test. The number of correctly solved tasks of groups one and two were almost identical, regardless of the prediction that the subjects were facing a future of healthy social bonds or a future with recurring health problems. Not even the prospect of a bleak future with regular hospital visits had a measurable impact on the results of intelligence tests. However, with the third group, for whom Baumeister predicted social loneliness and a repeated loss of connectedness, it was different. The cognitive abilities of this group decreased significantly during the test. The ratio of correct answers was about 27 percent lower.

Only a year later, another team of scientists discovered what happens in our brains during these moments. Naomi Eisenberger and Matthew Lieberman of the University of California, experts in social neuroscience, with social psychologist Kip Williams of Purdue University, described which activities they discovered in the brains of people who feel excluded. Findings like these help us understand why mental capacities decline so strongly and what happens to people in companies when they lack connectedness and belonging.

Williams developed a virtual ball game: the so-called »Cyber Ball.« One of the players has the experience of being excluded from the other players. During the game, all participants are in a functional magnetic resonance imaging (fMRI) brain scanner. With the help of this highly sophisticated scanner, the researchers could observe the brain activity of each player during the game.

Imagine you were one of those participants. During the experiment, you are in a massive brain scanner. In the device is a small monitor on which you can see yourself as a little man with two other players. You have a joystick in your hand. The researcher tells you that the two guys represent two other individuals in similar experiments. Now, they play ball with you.

The experiment begins. Merrily, you throw the ball to each other, while the researchers observe your brain activity. Once you have thrown the ball on the screen back and forth seven times, the game suddenly changes: The other two males throw the ball exclusively to each other. During the next 45 throws, you can only watch as the others play together, but you can't participate. Then the trial ends.

In reality, those other two little men were computer simulations, but the test subject did not know this. The scientists observed the activity of the brain during those last 45 throws. The moment you realised you were excluded, your dorsal anterior cingulate cortex (dACC) responded. This part of your brain is also active when you feel physical pain.

> The realisation: Our brain uses the same neural networks to process the loss of connectedness as it uses to process physical pain.

Modern brain research proves what we, as humans, seem to have known intuitively all along. Our language uses the same words for emotional disconnection as it uses for physical pain: Broken bones – broken heart. Shoulder ache – heart ache. Injured thumb – hurt feelings.

Why does the human brain use the same neural networks to process both physical pain and disconnection from others?

Numerous trials and years later, Naomi Eisenberger describes their findings as follows: »Human beings are born without the ability to feed or to defend themselves. We depend entirely on the people who take care of us. Our social belonging is, so to speak, taken piggyback by our neural pain system. It borrows the pain signal when a social relationship is at risk.« In other words, if a baby feels abandoned, it starts to cry – the brain gives him the same signals as if it had experienced physical pain. In those early years, this helps us get the attention and care we need from our environment for healthy physical and emotional development. Those experiences of our early childhood imprint on us and accompany us for the rest of our lives. A widower of advanced age can still perceive the loss of his spouse as physical pain.

The Cyber Ball studies by Eisenberger, Lieberman, and Williams revealed another interesting finding. Even though the largest activity of the dorsal ACC was observed when the tested person was actively excluded by the other persons, another experiment activated this part of the brain. Put yourself, once again, into the following situation: You are in a fMRI, looking at a monitor and holding the joystick expectantly in hand. The two other figures are playing with each other, yet you cannot join in. The researcher has staged the entire situation, so you feel unable to get involved. He turns to you and says, »We have a few technical difficulties, but we will solve that in a tick.« If someone, at that point, asked you if you felt left out, most likely, you would say, »No, it's all good.« At least, that's how most participants responded. However, your brain portraits reveal something else: The fMRI registered increased activity of your dACC! Your brain perceives not only pain when you lose your sense of belonging, but the neural pain areas are already active when you may not participate from the very beginning.

Gardeur | Back to success

It's December 2014 in Mönchengladbach, and the temperatures are already below zero. Nevertheless, Ellen Delbos is pushing me out the door. She wants to present the new façade with the colourful pants. »Previously, we could just as well have been a machine factory. The house was a solid grey. Nowadays, you can see what we stand for« bubbles out of her. Our conversation started quite differently just an hour earlier. I asked about the recent past of the company. The otherwise very lively Ellen Delbos went quiet. »The years 2007 to 2010 were a hard time for me,« she says with genuine concern.

The now executive assistant's 26 years of service are not a rarity at the traditional company Gardeur. It was established in 1920, and by 1969, the Gardeur Collection represented the first brand of pants in Germany and could not be missed in any well-stocked wardrobe. In the first years of the new millennium, Gardeur aligned itself with the midfield. The former owner and manager, Günther Roesner, had an accident in the year 2004. For health reasons, he could not lead the company full-time anymore. When his children took different career paths, he and his wife sold the business. In 2008, he was in agreement with a financial investor as to who would take over the traditional brand and employed a CEO with business experience.

»Look at the fine art on the walls,« says Ellen Delbos. She is in her element – her flow of words is as brisk as her steps as she leads me through the company. »Back then, most of the paintings were taken down and brought to an auction house. That did not feel good.« Even though it was not financially necessary, the new boss wanted to make a point. Among the employees, there was hope that the new management would lead the brand and company back to success. »The hope was justified, but the confidence it would happen was missing,« says Ellen Delbos. Perhaps, confidence was lacking, because there were different opinions about the future strategic alignment. They were looking for a new CEO.

Company: Gardeur GmbH
Industry: Fashion, Trouser Specialist
Headquarters: Mönchengladbach, Germany
Established: 1920
Employees: 2,000
Website: www.atelier-gardeur.com
Noteworthy: Due to a brand core process, both the corporate culture and connectedness of the employees improved. The company quadrupled its net income.

Gerhard Kränzle was the man who took the helm in 2010, and a few years later, he became the principal shareholder. With his many years of professional experience – he had worked his way up from pants seller to the head of purchasing of big fashion chains – he established his own financing strategy. In 2013, he took over the majority of Gardeur's shares, while transmitting to the staff they were working in a family business, once again. A bold decision: At this time, Gardeur could look back on several years of declining sales. The entire textile industry was in a crisis; companies like Schiesser or SinnLeffers slid into insolvency, and the »Arab Spring« made it difficult to continue with the main production in Tunisia. Since Kränzle could not rely on unlimited financial resources, he focused on developing the best possible potential he had in his company.

»I had a good product and bright people,« he recalls. »I counted on both.« He initiated a brand core process, which led to the overall greater well-being of staff and improved finances.

»Our interconnectedness improved massively,« says Christina Esser, head of quality assurance. »Before, we employees lived like we were on an island. Now, we all work much better with each other.« Gardeur, for the first time in many years, achieved higher sales: The net income quadrupled.

»Look at the images of advertising campaigns from the noughties years,« head of communication Ulrike Mellenthin tells me, while showing me some of the ads. »Men with bare torsos on a ship, a woman with a horse in a stable, and a couple in the snow – it lacked the common denominator! The statement of our brand was unclear.« In his first few months in his new business, Gerhard Kränzle experienced similar things. »He spoke to many of us and asked a lot of questions,« Christina Esser recalls. Kränzle arrived at the following conclusion: Not only the external communication of the brand was diffuse. There were also different opinions as to what Gardeur represented as a company.

To be more successful and to rise from the midfield back to the first league, the staff needed one common mental picture of the company and its products. »What does the Gardeur brand stand for and what should it be?« Gerhard Kränzle was just over 100 days in office, as the recollection of the company started from its roots. Sixty-three employees from all departments and management met for a joint workshop. The topic of the first day was a look into the past. Kränzle had been able to convince the now-healthy pre-predecessor Dr. Roesner to be part of it all. »Dr. Roesner wanted to come for only two hours, but he and his wife remained all day,« says Ulrike Mellenthin. For many of those present, long-forgotten memories re-surfaced. »My father allowed me to apply for a job here, because he had Gardeur trousers in the cupboard,« said one staff member, who started with the company in the late 80's.

The warm fuzzy feeling that had arisen in many of the 63 participants quickly disappeared when they met a second time: Looking into the present was the central theme.

In recent months, Gardeur had a brand agency that accompanied the company and talked to employees and traders. The results were difficult to digest for the workshop participants. »We saw appalling photos of dealers using the Gardeur logo from different eras, or collections did not fit together any longer,« one member recalls. »That was the external image of Gardeur for the end users. That did not feel good.«

The management asked those present, »Is it okay if we all begin to change something?« With the exceptional approval of the entire work-force, the change started.

The staff set up seven working groups that dealt with the brand essence of Gardeur. Their task was to help the company regain its old glory.

»First, we got all the paintings back from the auction house,« Ellen Delbos remembers. She is part of a working group, called »Anchoring the brand internally.« Among others, the working group initiated the »open department day.« For one year, every department of the company had one day a month to present itself to the rest of the enterprise. Whoever was curious could put his name on a list and be assigned to one of the many visitor groups. Again and again, the departments presented a steady stream of colleagues, whose contribution added to the success of Gardeur. One executive told me the unique thing about it was the spokesperson was not the head of the department, but one of the employees, who would take the opportunity to introduce himself and his department. This helped many people within the company, who had been more in the background, be seen.

Christina Esser, who heads the project group, »Anchoring the brand internally,« adds: »The emotional connection greatly improved with the ›open department-day.‹« Eva Michely, Junior Product Manager Mens-wear, noted: »All employees were invited to work on the brand core process. Not only did the cohesion between us strengthen, but we gained more confidence in each other, and ultimately, the working environment has changed for the better.«

Another working group of the brand's core process took care of the management culture within the company. »In the 80s and 90s, Gardeur was accustomed to success. That led to the build-up of many little ›king-doms‹ within the enterprise,« says Anja Kiehne. She is responsible for the HR area, as well as Co-Head of the working group management culture. »With our working group, we wanted to create the condition that we all work as one great team.« In the first year, the working group analysed the status quo in the company. It carried out a mini employee opinion survey and personal interviews with selected employees. »How do you experience our leadership, and what do you want to change?« Or »What do you expect from your supervisor?« Those are some questions for the selected people to answer.

»We then had a very diverse group of line managers,« Kiehne recalls. »These were people of different histories and experiences. After our survey, we realised we had to create awareness of the management culture, on one hand, while training our executives, on the other.« Although sales and earnings from Gardeur continued to decline – when Kränzle took over, the company had an operating result (EBITDA) of minus 11.9 million euro – the company began to invest heavily in its own workforce. The external labour law attorney, with whom I once happened to share my taxi ride, told me while driving: »Many other companies confronted with such a crisis would have ›swung the axe.‹« However, Gardeur handled the situation differently. Although Kränzle dismissed executives, most of the other employees could keep their jobs. He invested in training. »I want my employees to work for their entire lives,« he explains. »I could obtain maybe another 5 to 8 million euro in sales alone. However, if we want to reach an additional 100 or 150 million euro, this can be achieved only by good employees and executives. And for them to develop well, I happily spend the money.«

From the management training, as well as from the working group »executive culture«, another long-term approach evolved: a company-wide feedback culture. For almost all training courses and workshops, Gardeur consistently introduced feedback structures. That means, when the seven core brand work groups meet, they provide detailed feedback for each other as part of their agenda. After every presentation, there is feedback in the form of: »That's what we liked« and »That's what we would like to improve.« At the regular meetings of the three directors with the fourteen members of the top management level, it gets even more detailed: Every participant receives public feedback. »At the beginning, this feedback could be uncomfortable, especially on this level,« says an executive. »But over time and, in particular, in the individual feedback, I was more accepting of the impulse for change.«

Since feedback should not only be constructive criticism, but also praise-affirmative, the working group considered something special for the entire workforce: The Praise Card. On colourful business cards, they wrote phrases, such as: »THAT FITS« or »THAT ROCKS.« (In the German language, ROCK means »skirt.«) On the back of the card is an empty space with the heading »The following behaviour is praised.

»The sender fills in a few personal words and then passes on the cards in person.

Every employee received three of these Praise Cards for his colleagues; every executive received 50. »Pay attention to good performance,« was the recommendation to managers and employees. »Some wondered from the beginning, ›I already tell my colleagues if they are doing something good. Why these cards?‹« Anja Kiehne recalls. »However, when the same people then suddenly received praise cards, they rejoiced like little snow kings. With the card, you have something you can put on the table or hang on the wall. This is an ongoing reminder.«

»I feel noticed and taken seriously with my work when I get feedback,« junior product manager Eva Michely says. »If it is constructive, I can develop more. However, equally important to me is the praise and appreciation that came with it. With those little Praise Cards, this is all much easier for us.«

The first 1,750 Praise Cards were gone after a few months. Meanwhile, all employees can pick up new cards at the front desk. Over 1,600 additional cards were distributed within a year. Sometimes, those praise cards are not just used within the business, but outside as well. One employee distributed those cards to the nurses at the nursing home, where his mother lives. The idea of the cards turned out to be a very simple, yet effective, way to make feedback acceptable at Gardeur. One very young, but encouraged, employee went to the head of the company and asked: »Mr. Kränzle, please, would you give me feedback on how I come across to you?«

»And how does this work the other way around?« I want to know during my last conversation with Gerhard Kränzle. »Do you get feedback from your employees, as well?«

»Yes, fortunately. I often get to hear that I appear dominant and ask too few questions. That I came across as dominant, I was not aware. Apparently, some people don't dare get close. I am working on it. I want to become more accessible. However, employees with fewer inhibitions tell me right to my face what I need to do differently and what an employee-soul needs,« he says mischievously with a Swabian accent.

»And what about ›asking questions?‹« I want to know.

»I often say how things can be done, rather than letting the employee find it out for himself. I still must learn to let go more, instead of always interfering. But at the moment, that strikes me as very difficult, because in my experience, most of the time, I just know how it is done. However, I know that great company growth can occur only if I let my employees work more independently. Through our feedback rules, my employees, however, keep reminding me if I happen to be too directive again.«

»So what else has changed through the feedback culture at Gardeur?« I want to know.

»Both departments I am leading grew closer by using the praise cards,« says Christine Esser. »The appreciation among themselves has increased.« Head of HR, Anja Kiehne, reflects: »We got one step closer to our desire, to be ›more team.‹ The management meetings are more efficient. Previously, they were lengthy and often terrible justification scenarios. This is thankfully over.«

Unleashing your spirit

If the need for belonging and connectedness is so deeply rooted in our brains that our brains interpret a lack of it as physical pain, the question begs to be asked: Is this process reversible? Through the »two-monkeys-in-a-cage« experiments, we know connectedness can reduce anxiety. In the state of connectedness, neuroscience has shown the bonding hormone oxytocin is docked to the amygdala, which soothes this central part of our fear system. Once the fear is reduced, the brain gets better access to those neural networks, which run the higher cognitive processes.

However, what happens to people in a normal, relaxed state? Would bonding (and belonging) also help increase cognitive abilities? Priyanka Carr and Gregory Walton of Stanford embarked on exploring this question. They investigated, in extensive experiments, what happens to people who believe they are working as a team. However, there was never genuine cooperation among participants; it was all about the *feeling* of connectedness. In those experiments, each participant had to solve a task by himself. Some of them, through clever manipulation by the investigator, got the impression they were working with somebody else. During the multi-staged experiments, motivation, remaining mental power, performance, and enthusiasm were measured. In all categories, in which participants thought they were working with somebody else, they achieved good results.

In a first experiment, Carr and Walton divided the participants into two groups. To group one, they said, »You are part of a test in which people work together to solve a puzzle.« Throughout the experiment, the participants repeatedly received information to intensify the feeling: »We are working together on a common goal.« The participants in group two were told: »You are part of a test in which people solve puzzles.« The feeling of togetherness was deliberately omitted.

The participants of both groups worked alone in a separate room on an unsolvable puzzle, based on the »four-color theorem.« They were told: »You do not have to solve the puzzle. Just work as long and as hard as you like.«

After several minutes, the investigator entered the room and gave the participants a piece of paper with a supposed »message« as to how this puzzle was to be solved. The difference between the groups: The message for the participants from group one was formulated in a way as if it were a memo from another team member. The subject got the impression that another team member was trying to help them. The message for group two was so formulated that it was evident it was a memo from the investigator.

In this first experiment, Carr and Walton measured the time each individual spent with the puzzle. While the average for group two was around 11 minutes and 30 seconds, amazingly, the average duration spent with the puzzle in group one was almost 50 percent higher: 17 minutes and three seconds –with identical tasks, identical conditions, and identical contents of messages! The only difference: Group one believed it was working cooperatively toward the task.

Did the participants from group one spend 50 percent more time with the puzzle, so as to not disappoint the rest of the team they thought they were working with? Carr and Walton asked them. Group one answered they thought the task was interesting, and that they were motivated. With group two, this feedback was rather sparingly given.

The realisation: If people believe they are working collaboratively on a common goal, their motivation increases. In addition, the task seems more attractive.

In further experiments, the researchers investigated the differences between the remaining mental strength of both groups. After the puzzle task, the participants were interviewed on how tired they felt. The group that thought they were working with others reported a 33 percent lower level of fatigue than group two.

To support these statements with accurate, measurable results, Carr and Walton asked participants to go through computer-based tests, whose results would uphold their personal assessments. The method used was the stroop-test.

In this test, four words in succession appear on a screen: »red«, »blue«, »green«, and »yellow.« Sometimes, the words appear with the matching colour, but sometimes, the word and the colour do not match. The word »blue« could display in red, green, or yellow. The task for the participants was to press one of the four coloured buttons that corresponded to the colour of the writing. If the word »blue« was displayed in the colour »red,« the participant had to press the red button. Perhaps, even just by reading the last few lines, you have noticed you have to concentrate harder, because in a short time, you received a lot of information you had to process simultaneously.

Group one showed a 38 percent faster response time than group two. The stroop-test results matched the personal assessments. Participants had more mental capacity and were less exhausted.

> The realisation: If people work jointly on a given task, their subjective and objective measures of fatigue lessen.

In yet another experiment, Carr and Walton changed the experimental setup to investigate the differences in the attention spans of the two groups. Participants had eight minutes to observe a visually complex picture in which 18 objects were hidden. The tasks consisted initially of detecting those 18 subjects and then recalling them from memory.

Since 1974, several research results showed a connection between memory and attention. From the results of these experiments, Carr and Walton could derive an immediate difference, regarding the attention spans of the two groups.

After a few minutes, like before, all participants received a piece of paper with a message. Again, group one in this experimental arrangement received a message that made them believe they were working jointly. Group two received an official message from the researchers and concluded they were working alone.

To no surprise, group one achieved better results both in detecting the hidden objects and in subsequently recalling them from memory. They had a 12 percent higher hit rate.

> The realisation: When people feel they are working jointly on a task, their attention span increases.

A quick way to more connectedness

Organisations with a human-centred corporate culture develop various ways to allow connectedness to arise. Through my work with several companies, I have observed many different and equally functioning methods. An approach emerged, which is always effective, no matter the level of development of the organisation – a consistently deployed feedback culture. A culture in which clear feedback rules are implemented daily. A culture in which executives and employees openly meet either to give or receive feedback. A culture in which feedback happens, not just on the same level or downwards, but upwards, and free of fear.

I experienced many companies in which a real, serious, carried-through feedback culture led to a measurable difference for employees and executives – just as happened at Gardeur. A good measurable example I experienced in a DAX company was when, with organisational and HR developers, we selected one business area where I introduced brain-oriented feedback structures. Within a year, the employee opinion survey showed significant positive differences between the employees who were part of the feedback culture and the rest of the workforce.

What happens to people in companies where there is no such feedback culture? Nelson Mandela aptly summed this up in the following statement: »Resentment is like drinking poison and then hoping it will kill your enemies.«

If a colleague during a team meeting shuts me up and I get angry about that for the rest of the day, or go the rest of the week without addressing it, who's got the problem? Who's drinking poison, in this case?

Anyone who has ever been in a situation, where he felt hurt, angry, not seen or unrecognised, knows: In these situations, you do not feel connected to the other person.

For a moment, think of someone to whom you would like to say something – something crucial to you. So far, you have not addressed this issue. Perhaps, you are thinking of your partner, your neighbour, your boss, your colleagues, your mother, or your father. Now, assume you have told this person your concern. How much better would you feel?

One executive described the change in the feedback culture after a few months like this: »I can focus much more on my work, because I no longer carry so much baggage with me.« His colleague added: »I experienced feedback as a very powerful tool through which our confidence to one another improved significantly.«

If, in your company, all people were to give clear, respectful, brain-friendly feedback … how would the long-range bonding change?

Essence for Executives

Belonging – People want to feel connected

- Connectedness is a basic neurobiological need. Successful leaders create, in times of crisis, a high degree of affiliation to stabilise their employees.
- In times of anxiety and stress, connectedness acts as a sedative. If people perceive belonging, the brain secretes neurotransmitters that reduce the activity of the neural fear system.
- If people perceive the loss of belonging, the same neural networks in the brain become active, as if it were physical pain. Imagining the loss of belonging decreases the results by up to 27 percent, according to a well-known study.
- The less fear people perceive, the better they can use their prefrontal cortex, where the higher mental abilities are processed and, therefore, (are more likely) to develop their potential. »We had a sales growth

of 40 percent,« Phoenix Contact managing director Gunther Olesch remembers at the end of the worst crisis in the company's history.

- In an experiment, the assumption to be working in a team increased performance willingness by almost 50 percent and performance capacity by 12 percent. Moreover, scientists documented 33 percent lower fatigue.
- A consistently deployed feedback culture is one of the most efficient ways to increase belonging significantly within an organisation. »Our connectedness has changed massively,« says Gardeur Quality Assurance Chief Christine Esser. The net profit of the company quadrupled.

Chapter 3

Development and co-creation –
Human beings want to get involved

»Employees are much smarter than their bosses in German boardrooms often believe.«

Heribert Gathof, CEO, Eckes-Granini Germany
from 2000 to 2014

If a child must choose between toy building blocks and chocolate, what do you think it chooses? Many adults think it's the chocolate. They are mistaken. Most children opt for the blocks, and follow one of the deepest impulses we, as humans, carry inside us: the need to develop and co-create.

This need arises early. During the first weeks and months after we were born, many of us had a social environment that commented on our progress excitedly. »Look here! The little one smiled at me!« Or, »How cute! She took her first steps today!« At some point, we began to talk. We learned how to write, read, use a telephone, make a PowerPoint presentation, and complete a job application or, perhaps, even an annual balance sheet. We continued to grow beyond ourselves; we unfolded and shaped our environment.

Especially in the first years of our lives, this was not a cognitive process. Most of us don't remember our first steps, and hardly any toddler thinks, »Oh, today, I have especially grown beyond myself.« It's rather an experience from which a part of our brain deduces at an early stage: »Development and co-creation are part of this. If that is missing, something is wrong.« Gerald Hüther, therefore, referred to this »growing-beyond-oneself and developing ability« as a neurobiological basic need.

In a study conducted in cooperation with Judith Rodin in a nursing home in 1976, Harvard professor Ellen J. Langer described how people's lives are affected if this basic need is no longer met. When I mentioned

Langer's and Rodin's results in a lecture at a leadership conference of a life insurance company, the management team asked me afterwards to send the studies. The gentlemen could hardly believe it and had to see the numbers in black and white. A few days later, the company thanked me for the »amazingly clear« results.

How was this study conducted? The two scientists wanted to find out, with an experiment, whether it is possible to influence the aging process of nursing home residents. Is it possible to slow down the decline of health, alertness, and activity, or even reverse it? In a selected home, volunteer participants were divided into two groups: The experimental group was allowed, throughout the course of the study, to design their daily lives; the control group was told they hardly had to worry about anything, because the staff would take care of everything. The members of the experimental group had to take care of a houseplant. It was their decision to find a location in the room for it; they were responsible for watering the plant as well. In the control group, however, the staff placed the plant in the room and watered it.

Langer and Rodin encouraged the experimental group to design even more areas of their lives; they could choose where they received their visitors and what movies they wanted to see at what time.

After 18 months, significant differences were observed between the groups; the members of the active group saw improvements in their health, social activity, and general alertness.

The biggest surprise, however, came when comparing the number of surviving group members. The mortality rate of the residents with more design options was 50 percent lower than that of the control group!

If the neurobiological basic need for development and design is no longer met, a dramatic impact on our health may occur. The Whitehall studies, in which over 10,000 British civil servants were studied and which will be discussed in more detail later, proved this concept also applies to working life.

However, let us first look at the sunny side to understand what happens to people and companies when development and design are encouraged. At the beginning of the new millennium, the fruit juice manufacturer Eckes-Granini Germany started, step by step, letting its workforce co-design. Topics such as corporate strategy, which were previously the responsibility of top executives, were increasingly taken over and solved by staff. The measurable results were impressive, even after a short time.

Eckes-Granini Germany | The C.I.A. strategy

In 1996, Eckes-Granini Marketing Manager Heribert Gathof received the first impulse for more creative freedom in his company at the Croisette in France. What the Academy Awards are for the movie industry, the annual »Festival of Creativity« in Cannes is for the advertising industry. As usual, at such events, Gathof exchanged business cards with many people. One card he received from the owner of a film production company was extraordinary. The company called itself »C.I.A.« In Nieder-Olm, Gathof took the card repeatedly in his hands. »I found the name C.I.A. and what it stood for fascinating,« he recalls. »I wanted something just like that.« Gathof spoke with peers from his leadership level and convinced them to set up a »secret group« within the company. »In 1996, some of my colleagues and I felt like something fundamental had to change,« he recalls. »Before the management brings in consultants from the outside, we can also internally develop new strategic concepts.« This was the founding idea. To give meaning to the whole thing, Gathof produced business cards imprinted with »C.I.A.« (Change Infiltration Agent) for the six-member »secret force.«

»Looking back, our sense of identity greatly changed when we mutually pressed our cards in each other's hand. That was very powerful,« Gathof recalls. The new team came together several times for »conspiratorial meetings.« Together, they discussed what needed to be changed in the company, so revenues and mood brightened again in the medium and long term. The C.I.A. group developed both product suggestions for expanding the business base to bordering areas of operation (in addition to fruit juice, also fruit beverages and soft drinks), as well as a refocus on the company. A core topic was »focus on the market, rather than the preoccupation with internal structures and processes.«

With the results, Gathof knocked on the door of his boss. »That was a queasy feeling. We clearly had been working beyond our competence with developing this proposal. We had partly taken over the tasks of our boss, and I did not know what his reaction would be.«

It was agreed upon to present the thesis paper in a neutral place. The first meeting of the C.I.A. group with Gathof's boss took place in a conference room at the Frankfurt Airport. »I saw him making small checkmarks next to almost every thesis and he nodded.«

The C.I.A. group had proposed that the company's business development should be more driven through the product, rather than the research department.

Company: Eckes-Granini Deutschland GmbH
Industry: Fruit juice producer
Headquarters: Nieder-Olm, Rhineland-Palatinate, Germany
Established: 1857
Employees: 600
Website: www.eckes-granini.de
Noteworthy: The employees co-create the company's strategy and achieve a revenue-growth of 70 percent.

The C.I.A. group received the support of senior management for its previously secret work. Almost all developed theories were introduced by Gathof and his boss at the next executive board meeting and then transferred to an official strategy process. »A few months later, our C.I.A. group could see how basic things changed in the company, and we were part of this.«

The freedom to co-create had not been granted by management in the early years of the former marketing director. Gathof and his colleagues had seized it with courage. All participants knew they were exceeding their limits, but they followed their basic need for development and co-creation.

His experience in the C.I.A. group inspired Gathof when he became CEO of the newly founded subsidiary Eckes-Granini Germany, three years later. »There are only a few CEOs that can lead well and, at the same time, are great visionaries,« Gathof says with conviction. »As a CEO, one has to be honest with oneself. Therefore, I often put myself in service for those who developed such strategies, which we, as the management, would have never thought of. And these are usually not individuals, but groups. Employees are often much smarter than their bosses in German boardrooms believe.«

Eckes-Granini Germany | From C.I.A. to OMD

In his new position as CEO, Gathof launched, this time officially, a C.I.A.-succession project, named Operation Millennium Germany (OMD). The name says it all, because the national company, Eckes-Granini Germany, was founded at the beginning of the new millennium.

»It was the task of OMD, from the beginning, to develop strategic recommendations for the management,« says Sales Director Corinna Tentrup-Tiedje.

Unlike a strategy division or department, the OMD team is called together in always-new compositions for the solution of a specifically described problem. »When the management comes to a crossroads, it selects 30 to 50 people, works out a briefing, and lets the team search for solutions,« says Tentrup-Tiedje. The selection criteria for an OMD team include: Who is an expert for the current subject matter? Who is affected? Who is a maverick?

»What happens if the OMD team provides proposals the management does not consider as useful?« I ask in one of the many conversations. Gathof thinks for a while. »That has not happened a single time,« he replies.

The OMD idea had its debut in 2001. »Where do we want to be in 2005?« was the central question the management asked the OMD team. The interdisciplinary team, comprising members from all company levels, clearly recommended after several months of research and discussion: We must move away from glass bottles. »I, as a sales assistant and OMD member, was assigned the responsibility to intensify contact with politicians and find out from which way the wind was blowing,« says Tentrup-Tiedje. »We knew early on that it's only a matter of time before the glass bottle deposit was introduced. This would have undermined our business model.«

»Our OMD team, therefore, recommended the development of new PET filling machines,« Gathof recalls. »One plant cost 15 million euro – and we needed several of them! However, the recommendation was so thoughtful and conclusive that I set out to get the budget from headquarters and from the family owners.«

»Some colleagues thought we were crazy. With this idea, we turned the whole company upside down,« adds Corinna Tentrup-Tiedje. »Ultimately, within three years, we switched from glass to PET bottles, first with the product *Granini*, then with *hohes C*. We were able to solve our environmental concerns when it became clear the new bottles would come back as granules via the council's curbside recycling collection, and could be re-used.« Then another strength of the OMD idea became apparent. Because employees from almost every department were involved in the OMD strategy, their own colleagues could resolve any doubts within the workforce.

»At the time, I felt almost no resistance at Eckes-Granini Germany,« said Gathof. He feels confirmed in his idea of participation. »The employees, who had helped with the change to PET bottles, became important ambassadors for this new direction. It was not a requirement that came ›from above,‹ but an idea that was developed jointly.«

CFO Wolfgang Nickles is also happy. »Once we had implemented the change to the new bottles, revenues shot up by 70 per cent and more. Today, we are number three in the market of non-alcoholic beverages, right behind Coca-Cola and Pepsi.«

With this positive experience, the OMD became a constant model. Whenever management cannot find a solution to certain questions, it draws from the »wisdom of the crowd« (Gathof) and appoints a new OMD. »In recent years, when the commodity prices for oranges exploded, and we thought about price increases, we employed several OMD teams simultaneously, because a lot of strategic questions had to be solved,« recalls Tentrup-Tiedje.

»Do the employees not feel burdened by the overtime of an OMD? There is still the daily business!« I ask doubtfully at several places.

»The opposite is the case – participating in an OMD has always been an honour for me,« says Tentrup-Tiedje, who knows the required teamwork, both in her previous role as an employee, as well as in her new role as a boss. »It reduces the distance to the Board, and you reach an entirely different sense of community. Once, we did not have OMDs for an extended period, and the staff began actively to ask about it.«

Why we love Ikea

Eckes-Granini Germany achieved measurable revenue growth, using the basic neurobiological need for development and co-creation. The employees are now so happy in their work environment that fluctuation is low. I was a guest at the annual staff meeting and saw, by looking at the enthusiastic workforce, that a special culture prevailed.

In 2011, three scientists underpinned the fact that the approach of »development and co-creation« can also succeed in other companies.

Michael Norton of Harvard Business School and his colleagues, Daniel Mochon and Dan Ariely, published the results of extensive experiments that investigated the so-called »Ikea effect.« They prove that, when people get involved in co-creation, they measure their own work as being of higher value.

Imagine I offer you five euro for assembling a simple storage box from Ikea. I offer the same amount to your colleague, so he can unpack and check an identical storage box already assembled.

Afterwards, I ask you and your colleague how much money you would pay for each box. What do you guess?

In the experiments, the people who assembled the storage boxes would pay a price on average 63 percent higher.

Norton carried out further experiments that pointed in a similar direction. Imagine you receive, from me, origami paper and folding instructions for a frog or the traditional origami crane. Following up, I ask you to price your figure between one cent and one dollar. After you have left the room, I ask a group of people to look at your origami figure and assign a price between one cent and one dollar. In Norton's experiments, almost always the same thing happened: The creator of the figure, in this case you, would assign a price on average five times as high as the price assigned by the neutral group.

The realisation: When their neurobiological basic need for co-creation and development is met, people assign much higher importance to the results of their own work. What would be possible in your company if its people gave their work more importance?

Recently, I received a call from the CEO of an organisation close to the government, who had been part of the audience of one of my lectures months earlier. He asked me to speak at the annual employee event. I agreed and was able to convince him not only to facilitate the speech, but to have a large group with the entire staff afterwards.

On the day of the lecture, we allowed all employees, in alternating small groups, to reflect on the content of the presentation and to apply it to their professional lives. It was a dynamic afternoon with a lot of specific and often similar ideas presented to the Executive Board of the workforce. Similar to the OMD idea of Eckes-Granini Germany, all employees felt they were part of a change they helped co-create.

However, when I came into contact with the organisation sometime later, I found the CEO had committed the cardinal sin: The results worked out by the workforce had disappeared, with no comment, in the drawer of the boss. With this behaviour, executives miss out on a great opportunity! When people see their ideas have no effect, and therefore no sense, the impulse of wanting to co-create disappears. Unlike Sisyphus, we want to see the results of our work. If that is missing, in the long term, it results in a perceived lack of design options and may even make people sick.

In 1985 and 2000, in the so-called »Whitehall II studies«, the University College London examined 10,308 administrative employees in England. Most participants were working in London and were between 35 and 55 years old. Two-thirds were men. Hans Bosma, now a professor of social epidemiology at Maastricht University, evaluated the results: Men and women with low levels of design possibilities (low job control) became sick significantly more often than did those with high levels of design possibilities. The likelihood of heart disease increased by up to 80 percent!

Now, not every employee will die if his idea disappears in the boss's drawer or trash. However, the Whitehall studies point in the same direction as Ellen Langer's experiments in the nursing home: When people take the opportunity to co-create, a positive impact on their health can be noted.

Police Directorate Braunschweig | The stimulus of the workforce

At 11 o'clock on June 3rd, 1998, the first emergency calls arrived about the biggest rail accident in the Federal Republic of Germany. In Eschede, at track section 61, a high-speed ICE train derailed on the line between Hanover and Hamburg. This caused the deaths of 101 people. Over 2,000 workers from emergency services, fire brigade, army, and police were deployed. Many helpers came back from the deployment heavily mentally stressed.

»Our colleagues often experience extreme stress situations,« says Walter Kuhlgatz. He is now the director of health management for the Police Directorate Braunschweig, a department that deals with, among other things, supervising police officers after such traumatic experiences. Two years before the train disaster in Eschede, Kuhlgatz' colleague, Thomas Geese, was the creative nucleus that would sustainably improve not only the daily lives of Braunschweig colleagues, but also all police officers in the state of Lower Saxony.

Kuhlgatz' colleague, Roland Remus, recalls, »What we introduced to the directorate back then, the hardliners called ›fluffy blanket seminars.‹« Kuhlgatz does not feel bothered by this mockery by colleaques. What we offered in 1997 was classic stress and conflict management training. The need was obvious – even if hardly anyone admitted it. Police officers are called to serious accidents, deaths, and violent clashes. Additionally, there are often also private problems. Because of shift work, we have above-average divorce rates. A lot of colleagues now live in patchwork families – another factor of tension.«

»Many of the hard-nosed cops didn't want something like that, back then,« says Kuhlgatz. »In 1997, many were still marked by a Kojak-image. Dealing with stress did not fit the self-image of many of my colleagues.«

His colleague, Thomas Geese, had a keen sense of the growing demand on the police. Geese is now spokesman for the Police Department Braunschweig; in 1996, he initiated the idea Kuhlgatz implements today. »I got on the nerves of some executives, back then,« Geese says. »We were in the aftermath of a police reform and were in the midst of an upheaval. It was clear the country's police academy wanted strongly to reduce important things like behavioural training. At the same time, the need for such issues would continue to rise sharply.«

Company: Police Directorate Braunschweig
Industry: Police department
Established: 1814 / current structure since 2004
Employees: 3,000
Website: www.pd-bs.polizei-nds.de
Noteworthy: A nucleus of some engaged employees develops a coaching-offer for colleagues. This idea becomes bigger and, eventually, ends up in health-management for all officers in the state of Lower-Saxony.

Geese stayed persistent and was, ultimately, introduced to Heinrich Wahlers, the former director of the police of the county government. Wahlers has long passed the sceptre, but can still remember the earlier years when I visited him on a cool August afternoon. »At that time, I felt that my staff recognised a phenomenon of the time,« he says. »Something like I could not have imposed from the top of the organisation. These issues must come from the heart, and Thomas Geese instigated that at the right time.«

Although Heinrich Wahlers already had 3,500 personnel, he had to fight hard with the Interior Ministry for funding for a few additional positions. »But I had support from my team and was convinced they knew what they were doing. In retrospect, I'm still amazed at how such a small idea turned into such an avalanche.«

In 1997, Heinrich Wahlers achieved the approval for six officials, who formed a so-called coaching centre. This was a bold move at the time, as the shortage of personnel was already an issue. The task of the unit was to develop and implement training and coaching services for police officers. These included classical management training and a continuing education program for developing personal and social skills, such as conflict resolution discussions among colleagues or the ability to deal with their own stress.

In the neighbouring town of Wolfsburg, automotive giant Volkswagen was already working with a well-equipped team of coaches, who took care of leadership, team development, and efficiency issues – all that was in vogue at the time. Thomas Geese was able to establish contact with the Wolfsburg coaches. »For us, this was a good opportunity to learn how the free economy deals with coaching,« recalls Kuhlgatz. The police officers from Braunschweig drove to Wolfsburg and could get a taste of the coaching world of Volkswagen.

The staff of the coaching centre accomplished the development of the in-house expertise quickly. It was more difficult to generate a demand for the new offer internally. Across the whole police directorate the new team was trying to inspire some of its 3,500 colleagues for their own work. »We had to fight with the ›fluffy blanket image‹ and had had our work cut out to stand our ground against the internal resistances. Fortunately, we had a boss at the very top who supported the idea,« says Kuhlgatz.

»After the rail accident in Eschede, we realised in a brutally clear way that we had begun the right thing a year before,« says Roland Remus. »At the same time, we realised, in addition to stress and conflict management, we must also have trauma processing on the agenda.« Remus looks after the organisational development of the police department and supported the coaching centre idea from the beginning. Other colleagues were trained as coaches and trainers. Some specialised in trauma support, while others became mediators, supervisors, and systemic consultants.

The idea of a coaching centre from colleagues for colleagues paid off. »The courage in the police department to get involved in the soft subjects increased over time,« says Roland Remus. He has since trained in systemic constellation work. Today, he provides so-called systemic constellations workshops in the police department Braunschweig. »Especially, the colleagues with patchwork families can benefit from this method to resolve tension,« he says.

Under the new police chief, Harry Döring, the small nucleus of the coaching centre developed into a »Regional Advisory Board« in 2004. Döring recalls, »Our managers in staff positions would have never recognised the specific need and responded to it like the colleagues at the base were able to do. If that had not happened at the bottom, I do not know if it would have ever come from above. At least, it would have taken many more years.« The now-larger team could also take care of things like substance abuse counselling and occupational safety.

The initiative of the Brunswick police officers got around to the Interior Ministry. Even the police officers in the state exchanged views with each other. »Through Castor assignments (the joint protection of nuclear waste transport in northern Germany), there was a lot of cooperation between the different police directorates. In this context, the colleagues also wanted to know more about our coaching centre,« says Harry Döring. The creative impulse of a small team from Brunswick quickly became the role model for an entire state. All police departments in the state of Lower Saxony established their own »local counselling centres« and fulfilled a great need of police officers across the state.

Eckes-Granini Germany reached undeniably strong sales growth with the approach of the design. A small nucleus of the Brunswick Police Presidium changed the police work of an entire state.

Whether commercial enterprise, authority, or any other organisation, whenever teams can co-create their own work environments, people develop unimagined potential, and that applies to managers and employees.

Development and co-creation | Three ways to more stress resistance

Imagine you leave the house full of energy in the morning, pulling the door shut behind you. At this moment, you remember your house and car keys are still lying on the kitchen table and no one is home. To make matters worse, the USB stick with the presentation you are to give in 30 minutes is still in the study room.

Within fractions of a second, parts of your neocortex and limbic system activate control centres in the brainstem. At various points in your body, norepinephrine and epinephrine are released. You are in the first phase of a stress reaction. There are two ways to respond.

One possibility is a so-called uncontrollable stress response, leading to a cascade-like activation of the HPA (hypothalamic – pituitary – adrenal) axis and, ultimately, to the secretion of cortisol from your adrenal glands. This entails physical reactions, such as rapid pulse and elevated blood pressure and blood sugar levels. You will find yourself in classic fight, flight, or freeze mode quickly. That's not a very favourable condition under which to solve complex problems.

Another possibility is a controlled stress reaction in which the HPA axis activation, the secretion of cortisol and all related physical reactions don't appear. The good news is you will not get into a fight, flight, or freeze mode, but you will retain access to your cerebrum, especially the wonderful prefrontal cortex. This is the area where most of your potential is hidden and which will help you solve problems.

There are three ways to cope with challenging stressful situations in the favourable state of the controllable stress response. It is usually sufficient if one of these three ways is accessible, but would be ideal if all three were available to you.

1. You have the firm belief you will find a solution to the problem by yourself. In our example, you might remember you have previously opened a cellar window from the outside. You believe you can gain access to your house this way.

For a company, this means: Employees who experience a high level of design and development reach a state that Canadian psychologist Albert Bandura calls »Mastery Experiences.« In this state, the belief grows that one will find solutions for future problems.

The neuroscientist, Amy Arnsten, summarises the findings of her colleague, Steven Maier: »Often the mere illusion of being able to solve a problem is enough to continue to receive access to the prefrontal cortex.« The more employees are allowed to co-create, the more the belief in their own abilities strengthens. This increases the probability these people will show a controlled stress reaction in challenging situations and retain access to their full potential.

2. You trust other people can help you solve the problem. In our example, you may ask a neighbour to give you a ride to the nearby workplace of your partner, who has an additional key to the front door.

For a company, this means: Managers who believe employees can contribute to the resolution of problems, develop trust in this additional resource. This process must begin when the company finds itself in calm waters. Over and over again, I encounter boards whose business doesn't work anymore and can't develop a diversification strategy themselves or with their departments. These managers are often in a state of deep unrest, and they try to integrate their own workforces at the last minute. Often, however, this attempt fails, because they are no longer in a position at this late stage to build the confidence in the solution-finding skills of their workforce. How are they supposed to do it, anyway, if they lack a previous positive reference experience they could have made with their staff? The following applies: The more a manager lets his employees co-design at an early stage, the more consolidated the confidence of the bosses in their own teams. The probability increases that bosses show a controlled stress response in challenging situations and continue accessing their full potential.

3. Even if you don't yet know how the problem can be solved, trust there will be a good solution. In our example, you might remember you have forgotten the key before and could always get inside the house. This happened to the Phoenix Contact Managing Director, Prof. Gunther Olesch, during the crisis of 2009 (see chapter 2). Olesch recalls other difficult periods, which he had previously experienced and ›survived‹ during 2009. This reference experience helped him trust there would be a solution for the year 2009.

For a company this means: Pay attention to the people who cannot provide picture-perfect CVs. These employees have a special competence: The breaks in their CVs and the »always picking themselves up again« have blessed them with the experience that, somehow, things will go on. The personnel manager of a Nordic energy group captured this briefly at a global change workshop: »We are a company that has never struggled with resistance since its establishment. We have always earned a lot of money. Now that the energy market is turning, we lack the experience to deal with difficulties.« The more employees with diverse backgrounds can design together, the more cumulative experience expertise is available in the workforce. Albert Bandura calls this »Social Modeling« – people who look at a situation as hopeless benefit from the confidence of others and regain access to their potential.

Gathof and his leadership team reached measurable results in a 70 percent revenue growth and other strategic advantages with the OMD. »Why did you limit the cooperation with the OMD team to the management and a few selected key positions?« I asked.

»The OMD structure is tailored in its form to support the management for strategy development,« says Gathof. »For the advice and support of the middle and lower levels of the company, we have other ideas that fit better. Of course, we also use the ›wisdom of crowds‹ and theme ›participation.‹« The manager grins. »It's just not called OMD any longer, but Enterprise.'«

»Our management philosophy is simple,« explains Martin Gehr, who heads the Department of Business Development. »We are convinced people already carry a lot of solutions in themselves. Our job is to ensure the employees of different departments talk to each other more often and more intensively. It needs better networking to gain access to brainpower.«

If questions arise in the departments to which there are no easy answers, a group called »Enterprise« is formed in which the employees feel and act like entrepreneurs. »We had a specific situation with a trading partner,« recalls Marketing Manager Katja Gadanyi. »The fronts had been hardening quite a bit with this partner for some time. Due to the massive increase in commodity prices for oranges, we also had to increase our distributor's selling prices to remain profitable. This led to heated discussions with this chain.«

To find solutions for improving and redesigning the relationship with the trading partner, the management appointed nine employees for a new enterprise group.

»It is very important that the colleagues are from many different departments,« says Gadanyi. »We deliberately intend that colleagues think about things of which they actually have no idea. They should put on non-specialist glasses. In the case of the trading partner enterprise group, employees from sales, marketing, logistics, controlling, and IT were involved.« Gathof adds: »We knew about some of the participants ahead of time; they were lateral thinkers. Most of the time, those are the younger ones in the workforce. This is desired and wanted. Only in this way, we can leave the habitual ways of thinking behind.«

At the beginning of the trading partner Enterprise group, there were expected irritations. »I am the one who should advise customers. What is the colleague from IT doing here?« was one piece of feedback. »In this situation, it was particularly important to ensure the ›experts‹ don't explain from where the wind blows to the people from other fields,« says Gadanyi. »All participants should work as free of known knowledge, ideas, or negative previous experiences as possible. This can lead to new approaches.« The initial irritation dissolved as the participants noticed the added value that the special group composition provided after a short time. »Well, I would not want to give up my IT colleague in the enterprise group under any circumstances!« the customer service representative later admitted. He had seen common ideas arise that were previously unthinkable.

Katja Gadanyi has also taken over the role of facilitator for the two enterprise groups, besides her tasks in marketing. She ensures the work of the group takes place within a clear allocation of roles and structures. She also abstains from content discussions. »I like this new job and get support from an external supervisor if it is needed,« she says. »In the group, there are always trends that participants want to take over the roles they have in everyday business. Then, it's my job, sometimes, to convince the controller to prepare a draft marketing concept. I am always fascinated about how different and how solution-focused the work in the enterprise groups is. If the group gets stuck, sometimes, I need only to adjust the process structures. Then suddenly, the blockage dissolves, and you can feel the wisdom of the crowd again.« In such moments, Gadanyi likes to change the question for the participants or the compilation of the subgroups during a meeting, or lets everyone do something different for a moment to change the direction of thought.

When speaking to the participants, I realised, after some time, the enterprise groups are anything but project groups. First, enterprise members are not to participate in their specialist functions, but are to take on special roles with which they are not familiar. Second, there is no time frame for interdisciplinary cooperation. »The enterprise group for the trade partner has existed for nine months, and there is no limit,«

reports Gadanyi. »It feels like we are in the middle of it. We have been going through various stages of development within the group, and I see a greater acceptance and appreciation among the participants. We have developed many concrete, content-related approaches.« With the developed ideas, Eckes-Granini Germany has performed more than 20 external conversations for future cooperation. The enterprise group discussed the new, roughly outlined approaches with the business partner and received substantial feedback. This significantly changes the relationship with the trading partner, because he feels like he is being taken seriously. »I think we will put together new enterprise groups for many other situations,« says Gathof.

Connected work, unfamiliar roles, permission to think laterally, a clear process structure, and plenty of freedom to co-create are parts of the recipe for the success of the enterprise idea. »The work results are partially outstanding,« says Gathof.

Gadanyi adds, »It affects me when I observe individuals develop differently in the enterprise groups from the daily business.«

»If we notice or suspect talents anywhere in the company, we invite them to join such a group,« says Gathof. »Sometimes, these are even trainees. Then they get the opportunity to show what they can do. The results are then quickly visible to us.«

Development and co-creation | The boss spares his brainpower

Consciously promoted development and co-creation has another major side effect: Executives who let their employees co-create can outsource thought processes, thereby unburdening themselves. This release will take place not only in major strategic projects, like Eckes-Granini Germany, but in daily exchanges, which is where it begins. I experience it regularly within my work when I teach executives the method of »brain-friendly communication.« Before long, the bosses report, »I have to worry less about what motivates my employees. They now tell me what they need to help them achieve their goals better.«

This mental relief is becoming increasingly important these days. The myth of multitasking has been refuted multiple times in recent years by scientific evidence. In 2001, Nelson Cowan, from the University of Missouri, demonstrated in extensive studies that most people can simultaneously keep only a maximum of four pieces of information in their consciousness. Harold Pashler, from the University of California in San Diego, supported this with his experiments: If adults are given two simple tasks at the same time, each task demanding only a minimum of cognitive performance, the time the adults need to solve the tasks doubles. The mental performance of an adult is reduced to that of a schoolchild.

Our prefrontal cortex works serially. This means it can do only one thing at a time. Imagine you are in a meeting. A colleague speaks about a current project. Meanwhile, your boss pushes the printout of the latest quarterly figures across the table to you. At the same time, you answer some important emails on your iPhone, while thinking about what you need to do to get an employee to create an important presentation for the CEO tomorrow morning. While you believe you can do these things at the same time, your brain literally switches back and forth between the different neural networks in fractions of a second. There is a neural network that listens to the colleague, another for the quarterly figures, a third for the mail, and a final one for the thoughts about the employee.

The frequent activation and deactivation of various networks requires energy, a lot of energy. Over 80 clinical trials at the University of London have shown that people with such a high density of parallel stimluli temporarily lose up to ten intelligence quotient (IQ) points of their mental capacity. If you smoke a joint, you will lose only four IQ points!

For some executives, it is a great personal development task to permit more co-creation. They believe they will no longer be able to »properly control« their teams, without having tight specifications in place. We have been taught diverse methods and subcategories of »corporate governance« for decades. If one Googles this phrase, more than three million search results appear. Some bosses seem to derive control of their employees from the management of the company.

What is needed is a process of awareness. If executives still feel internal resistance about the topics of development and co-creation of their own teams and the workforce, it is mostly due to their internal pictures of themselves. Some bosses are still firmly convinced that »my employees work for me« and act accordingly.

Upstalsboom's head of HR, Bernd Gaukler (from chapter 1), has a different belief. »As a leader, you have to be aware that it is your job to lead people. This is not a privilege, but a service.«

Essence for Executives

Development and co-creation – Human beings want to get involved

- The neurobiological basic need for development and co-creation becomes based in humans through early childhood experiences. Successful executives use this natural driving force in their employees to achieve better business results.
- Eckes-Granini Germany had its staff help co-create the company's strategy. Subsequently, CEO Heribert Gathof could not detect internal disturbances or resistance during the implementation within the organisation. The company increased its revenue by 70 percent through this strategy.
- Development and co-creation influence health. When nursing home residents received more options during a study, their death rate decreased by 50 percent. A long-term study with over 10,000 British civil servants showed better health (for example, a significantly lower likelihood of heart disease), related to the ability to co-create.
- When humans co-create, they assign a much higher value to the results of their work. In an experiment in which a group of subjects solely unpacked Ikea boxes, while another group assembled independently, the »assemblers« would pay a price for the item 63 percent higher than that of the »unpackers.«
- Executives who let their employees co-create increase long-term confidence in their employees' competence. Through confidence in others, the stress resistance of the executive grows, as well.
- Multitasking is a myth. Our prefrontal cortex consumes considerably more energy when it needs to do several things at once. Thereby, people

temporarily lose up to ten points of their intelligence quotient (IQ). This is also confirmed in everyday business:

The more often an executive lets his workforce co-create – »outsourcing« thought processes to them and having to focus on fewer things – the more access he retains to his own brain potential.

Chapter 4

Trust – People need someone who believes in them

>The great trust of our CEO let our self-confidence grow.«

Lisa Timeus, student, Weleda AG

The piece of paper had it literally in itself. The paper of the advertising flyer, which the apprentices and students of Weleda used, had incorporated seeds. If readers buried the compostable paper in the earth, flowers would sprout from the ground.

In the summer of 2013, the students had established their own company: »Naturtalente (naturals) by Weleda.« A few months later, they brought to the market their own natural cosmetic product, which was sold in hundreds of drugstores. The concept of the incorporated seeds was just one of many innovative ideas.

»My experience with students is they can mature to the most valuable employees in the company if it is possible to unfold their existing potential,« says Ralph Heinisch. He is CEO of the natural cosmetics and drug manufacturer from Schwäbisch Gmünd, a small village that's a 40-minute car ride from Stuttgart. »This requires a pre-given operational framework, quasi the side-lines of a playing field. Within this context, one should let them work independently and give them the opportunity to create their own rules.« In summer 2013, Heinisch sat down with his apprentices and students and asked them to work together on a project. The Baden-Wurttemberg state horticultural show in Schwäbisch Gmünd was about to take place close to the German headquarters of Weleda. Heinisch proposed to the trainees that they participate in the show by representing the company. Exactly what they would do was up to them. After a few weeks, the students approached him with several ideas, including a barefoot path in the form of the Weleda logo, thematic cooking classes, and »four elements« workshops. After a joint discussion, the trainees and students decided amongst themselves to establish their own junior company. This process was new and a first significant experience. »I realised that to make this project happen, everyone had to work and think outside the box«, Heinisch told me. »The students would think and work in a much more complex [manner] than was possible if they stayed in their own specialist department. They could look at the project from a perspective that usually only the business owner or the CEO respectively has.« The students were looking forward to this challenge. »We got a lot of trust and confidence from Mr. Heinisch. That triggered a lot of the enthusiasm,« says the 20-year-old Alena Klinz.

With full conviction, Heinisch and the HR department of Weleda supported the trainees' and students' company. Antonia Jeismann, a staff member of the HR development department, managed the project and was the primary contact for the junior company. To make it worthwhile, the young entrepreneurs received 20.000 euro as starting capital. »Don't you think that's not much money to start your own company?« I asked Heinisch.

»Indeed, that's not much,« he replied. »At the beginning, however, neither the trainees nor we knew where the journey was taking us. Interestingly, it soon turned out that more money was not necessary. To the contrary!« The young junior company paid its own way. Naturally, they reached out for Weleda structures, which made things a bit easier. For example, they could use some existing business contacts, so they didn't have to build those from scratch.

Naturtalente by Weleda

»After the first workshop, after the starting shot, the trainees decided which departments and which roles their business needed,« says Antonia Jeismann. »In the same workshop, they also decided who would take on which position.« One of the selected start-up managing directors was just 18 years old and in his first year of apprenticeship. To support him in his position, Jeismann and her boss Dr. Isabella Heidinger gave him leadership coaching. »Initially, he was reluctant, but the other students trusted him with this position, and he has developed his potential in a short time,« says Heidinger.

A little later, the name of the young company was decided. Because, internally, the trainees were nicknamed »Naturtalente« (naturals), they took on this name without hesitation and called their company »Naturtalente by Weleda.«

»From the very beginning, it was clear to us we wanted to have a strong focus on values within our new company,« says start-up managing director Alena Klinz. »In addition to the departments of finance, marketing, and sales, we even built one to cover the topic of values,« she adds.

»What exactly is the task of the department of values?« I asked.

»For example, the trainees introduced the ›heart and souls circle,‹« says Klinz. »At the beginning of each meeting, everyone has the opportunity to say what's on their mind and how they feel. We noticed it is easier for us to talk about the substantive topics if we put something personal at the beginning.« Her colleague, Lisa Timeus from the values department, adds, »Of course, we could identify with the traditional corporate values of Weleda, but we wanted to recreate them in a young and personal way. We looked at it from two levels. On one hand, we looked at the values we implemented in guiding and shaping our cooperation in the junior company, how we wanted to deal with each other if, for example, someone made a mistake. On the other hand, we looked at how we wanted to deal with our product and its sustainability.«

Naturtalente by Weleda was not an independent company in a legal sense. Nonetheless, every trainee and student worked with great dedication and seriousness, as if it were a real business. »On average, the Naturtalente spent 20 percent of their time in the junior company,« says Antonia Jeismann. »Of course, there were also those individuals, who temporarily devoted 100 percent of their time.« Particularly challenging was the situation for the students. In the framework of their dual degree programm, they alternated 3 months at college and 3 months for pratical work at Weleda. Yet, some took a leading position in the junior company. Every manager had a deputy; therefore, every three months they had a complete hand-over to the next person. »Often, this was a masterpiece of organising,« Dr. Isabella Heidinger recalls. »Trainees often found these handovers very stressful. However, in retrospect, they told us how much they had learned about everyday life at Weleda.«

Company: Weleda AG
Industry: Pharmaceutical, cosmetics
Headquarters: Arlesheim, Switzerland
Established: 1922
Employees: 2,000
Website: www.weleda.com
Noteworthy: The trainees at Weleda built a company, sold their own (limited) products, improved the business relationship to one of Weledas most important b2b-customer, and improved their self-confidence.

The commitment to the junior company has not gone unnoticed. »Of course, like in any other business, we are human, too,« says Ralph Heinisch. »Some colleagues criticised [the fact] that the apprentices and students spent so many hours working outside the department. They wondered if that was necessary.« Some employees were also irritated that the junior company got so much attention from the CEO and the HR department. But the initial scepticism disappeared quickly. »I never expected the kind of support that suddenly appeared from the parent organisation for the Naturtalente,« says Ralph Heinisch. It came at the right time: The young entrepreneurs realised with what high ambitions they had started. »I was surprised you have to involve so many people in the development of a new product before it is ready to hit the market,« says Alena Klinz.

»You must spend a lot of time on the product testing and on dealing with the authorities,« adds Andreas Barth, one of three managers of the junior company. The members of Naturtalente by Weleda realised the manufacturing of their own product could not be done before the state horticultural show. They consulted with the parent company Weleda and got permission to re-introduce an existing product, the Calendula Plant Soap, but with a new name, new design, and new packaging. Later, after intensive preparation, the Naturtalente had this product produced themselves: a limited edition of 6,500 pieces of soap with the name ›Sonnenschatz (Sun Sweetheart)‹. Only the ingredients were the same as those in the known calendula soap; the rest was entirely new.

»The enthusiasm of the trainees for their junior company carried over to their specialist departments,« says Ralph Heinisch. The employees of Weleda and even the partner companies showed interest. »Our suppliers provided unpaid services for the junior company for which we would otherwise have had to pay,« Heinisch recalls. The new product eventually needed not only a new name, but also its own packaging and website. Even the stamp on the soap was redesigned to ›Sonnenschatz‹.

The parent company offered to take its own calendula soap off the shelf in its Weleda store at the state horticultural show, so only ›Sonnenschatz‹ was available. Success was not long in coming. First, the retailers from the region showed interest in the new product. However, the biggest coup the Naturtalente landed was when they met with the representatives of a large retail chain: Müller drugstores. The retailer was so excited that it immediately commissioned its own group of trainees to make the purchase negotiations with Naturtalente by Weleda. Apprentices met with apprentices as equals. The result: ›Sonnenschatz‹ was taken into the inventory of 500 Müller drugstores. »Since then, the relationship between the company Weleda and Müller drugstores has had an entirely different quality,« says Heinisch. »So far, the junior company is the largest project I've done in training,« he adds. »At the end of the training, we have a team that holds all the skills a company needs to be sustainably successful.«

»Through the fact that we were given so much confidence from the Weleda Management, each of us could develop high confidence during this time,« says Lisa Timeus. »To accept this great responsibility was very special.« Ralph Heinisch carries a deep confidence and trust in his students. »I learned that employees are capable of tremendous achievements if you show them trust and give them the necessary freedom.«

Heinisch knows that from personal experience. Ten years ago, the job of turnaround manager literally fell into his lap. Initially, he began his career as an area manager for a building materials company. However, this quickly ran into severe economic trouble. The owner gave Heinisch confidence. In him, they saw the skills to save the company, and they asked him to take on this task. »I didn't get any new employees or replace anyone. I achieved the turnaround with the existing team,« he says. »When I gave people space and responsibility to solve problems independently and gave them my trust, they grew beyond themselves.« Heinisch and his colleagues succeeded, in time, to bring the business out of the red. Since then, he has been regularly called to companies to help them get back on track – just as with Weleda, which generated an unexpectedly high loss in the year 2011. Now, the company is profitable again.

Fifteen months and 6,500 ›Sonnenschatz‹ soaps later, the junior company Naturtalente by Weleda closed its doors in December 2014. For future apprentices and students to feel the magic of ownership, the concept of the junior company has been made a regular, integral part of the training curriculum. With the trust given to them, many young people can grow beyond themselves.

The Circle of Potential | How humans grow beyond themselves

Why did Ralph Heinisch grow beyond himself when the owner of the building materials company put trust in him? Why did his staff succeed, just because he believed in them during the turnaround? What influence did the management of Weleda have on the Naturtalente through its trust? While working with managers and employees in companies, I devote a lot of time to preparation to be able to convey complex content quickly and memorably, later. Workshop participants have told me repeatedly that one specific model is noticeable for them: the Circle of Potential. With it, many aspects of successful leadership can be explained – as can the strong influence of trust on employee performance.

The model of the Circle of Potential, which I developed a few years ago, is based on the core assumption that every person holds a lot of hidden potential. But what does ›potential‹ mean?

Potential is something invisible, something not yet made visible – something you might develop. You know it from football when a commentator or the coach says, »The player has not accessed his potential.« The player did not show what was truly within him. In the corporate world, it's the same. There are the talented people, in whom you might see »a lot

of potential« or the executive who carries »potential for more« within himself. Perhaps, you also know of people or teams that suddenly »no longer display the potential« that is innate within them.

Based on personal experience, I would like to explain this Circle of Potential to you. At 23, I started my career at Sony Music. At first, I was building the online department of EPIC Records, a division of the entertainment company. In 2000, the online executives were still regarded as the renegades of the company. My boss Jörg Hacker, the managing director of EPIC Records, loved to show me off everywhere. I had been with the company for just three or four months when he – in his typical, slightly plainspoken manner – stepped into my office, filling the doorway with his massive, imposing size. »Purps, next week it's your turn to present the results you had so far in the info-meeting,« he said. Walking away, he had another thought: »And do not disappoint me.« You simply could not take offence from the somewhat crude former highway officer. We all liked him a lot.

The meeting he entrusted me with took place once a week. Jochen Leuschner, the president of Sony Music, met with all the company's managing directors, vice presidents, and directors, and with some employees who had significantly less impressive titles. They could all present their latest and most important issues. Because the music industry is fast-paced, a weekly exchange was indispensable. Most participants were at least two or three times my age. Our president was a big player in the European music industry. His greying hair and his friendly-but-slightly-distant manner were formidable.

After my boss had left my office and I realised what he asked of me, adrenaline shot through my veins. »Me, in this most prominent meeting of the company, where everyone presents their really cool products nonchalantly ... I'll be the baby among the adults,« I thought.

Look closely at the image of the Circle of Potential. At the level of my internal pictures, something changed: I developed several limiting, unfavourable pictures: »Me in this meeting ... that can't work! I won't be confident. They'll ask me questions I can't answer. This is gonna be embarrassing.«

The next day, I went to my boss and tried to convince him it was still too early for the presentation of my results in this prominent forum. However, he could not be dissuaded from his idea. »Purps, last week you presented in front of the sales team, and it was great,« he said. »I saw you, and you got positive feedback. I'm not worried. You're gonna rock it.« And with that, for him, everything was said.

Back then, my boss used a highly effective method: He believed in me. I was still nervous, but the fact that this remarkable (to me) man believed in me strengthened my internal pictures of myself and my belief in my own abilities. Once again, I got access to that which was lying dormant within myself: my potential.

If you look back at the Circle of Potential, you know what comes next: the behaviour. Back then, I prepared for the meeting with a clear head. Then, on the big day, I presented my results. I was reasonably calm. Although I was not quite as smooth as my older lecturing colleagues, at least I spoke well and had the right answers to all the questions. Now, the next level of the Circle of Potential took effect: the experiences. My experience was that I could manage this situation. I encountered far less negativity than what I had feared and was more relaxed than expected. The Circle of Potential closed. This pleasant experience generated new internal pictures: »I can manage a situation like this; I can cope with such a meeting and with all those much more experienced people.«

Two months later, my boss sent me to the same meeting, once again. With my encouraging experience and now-positive internal pictures, I prepared myself, so I was more relaxed and behaved distinctly confident. I collected even better experiences than before. My internal pictures strengthened, regarding my ability to cope with such situations.

Even though I can now formulate precisely these internal pictures, back then, I was not all that clear about them. This Circle of Potential takes place unconsciously, although it is highly effective. We can use the underlying patterns for ourselves, but also for the people around us by influencing them on all three levels: »internal pictures,« »behaviour« and »experience.«

In this chapter, I will talk specifically about what happens when we strengthen the level of internal pictures, just as CEO Ralph Heinisch did at Weleda with his Naturtalente, when he trusted them with their own company, and as I experienced at Sony Music, when my boss believed in me. Let us go a little deeper and explore what is possible when internal pictures are changed.

Strong internal pictures unfold our potential measurably

In 2001, psychology professor Joshua Aronson of New York University and Carrie B. Fried from Winona State University conducted a study with 79 Stanford students. Subtly, they strengthened the internal pictures of some participants and helped them to better their exam results.

The researchers divided the students into three groups. Some participants were told that the study comprised a one-time exchange of letters between a pupil and a university student. The pupils were each in a very difficult phase of their academic achievement, and the hope was that the encouraging exchange with the college students would help them overcome this phase. The story was fictitious. However, the researchers had prepared handwritten letters in sealed envelopes from alleged pupils in problematic personal stages of their lives. The experiment dealt with something entirely different: Aronson and Fried wanted to subtly change the internal pictures of the students, regarding human intelligence. They made sure the students of the test group grappled with the approach of a »stretchable/plastic intelligence.« This method assumes our intelligence is not a factor that cannot be influenced, but intelligence is variable and may be increased.

They gave the students these instructions: »Write to the pupils something about human intelligence. Because human intelligence is expansible, people can learn all their life – regardless of age. When pupils understand that, through diligence and hard work, their intelligence will increase, it is much more likely they will try to overcome their current problems.« Besides providing these instructions, the researchers showed students a film about the plasticity of the human brain and its intelligence. To strengthen the internal pictures of this approach to intelligence, the researchers also asked the students to add examples of their own experiences to uphold the theory of variable intelligence.

The students of the test group invested three hours in this experiment. During the first two meetings with the scientists, they each wrote a letter to a pupil. During the third session, they wrote a speech about changeable intelligence, which they recorded and to which they then listened. With this, the active influence of the researchers over the students was finished.

The two control groups received different tasks. One control group was also to contact another alleged pupil, with a single letter. However, they were influenced by an intelligence model which would not talk about expansive intelligence. The second control group participated only in some surveys.

Aronson and Fried observed the three groups over twelve months. Despite the relatively short duration of time (three hours) during which the internal pictures influenced the test students, the researchers could determine significant differences between the groups after one year. The concept of the variability of intelligence, which a year earlier the students gave to the pupils in those encouraging letters, were never intended for the pupils, but from the very beginning, for the students themselves. The resulting internal picture of »my intelligence is not limited, but expandable« influenced not only their personal well-being, but also their performance at the university.

After one year, the students in the test group reported high satisfaction with their studies. Measured on a scale system, their satisfaction was nine percent greater than those of participants, who assumed that intelligence was not expansible. The objectively measurable factors were encouraging: After twelve months, the students within the test group, which proceeded from a modifiable intelligence model, achieved better exam results by an average of seven percent.

You know from the model of the Circle of Potential what happened: Through their positive internal pictures, they could unfold a greater proportion of their potential. The result was that they developed a behaviour that helped them achieve better marks.

Six years later, Ute Bayer and Peter Gollwitzer at the University of Konstanz started another short-term experiment. Immediately after three minutes of influencing the internal pictures, students received a math test and scored higher than participants in the control group by 53 percent. Published in 2007, the study showed how rapidly potential can be awakened. Bayer and Gollwitzer had deliberately chosen forty women as test persons, because women struggle with the stereotypical prejudice that »women are bad at math.« The participants received ten minutes to solve fourteen math problems. The scientists divided them into two groups and asked them to memorise the following sentence three minutes before the test: »I will solve as many problems as possible.« The control group was asked to remember the following sentence within the same time frame: »And when I start with a new problem, I will tell myself: I can do it.«

During the following ten minutes, group two solved significantly more tasks. On average, group two managed 4.3 correct answers, compared with only 2.8 in group one. (The tasks were tough, Ute Bayer told me.) But why? The sentence »I will solve as many problems as possible« had no influence on the internal pictures of the participants. However, it is precisely those pictures which have to be stimulated. With Naturtalente by Weleda, Ralph Heinisch addressed the concept of faith in their own abilities. My boss at Sony Music did just the same: strengthening my faith in my own abilities.

The sentence »And when I start with a new problem, I say to myself:

I can do it,« strengthened participants' belief in their own abilities. Back then, the Stanford students were also convinced they could make a difference through own efforts: the quota of their own intelligence.

Try it for yourself: Think of a goal you want to achieve. Maybe you want to go jogging for 60 minutes twice a week, or you want to complete the doctoral thesis you started a few years ago, or the processing of a long-overdue strategy paper. Once you have found a suitable target, tell yourself these two sentences in your mind:

1. I will do the best to achieve this goal.
2. If I'm on my way to this goal, I know I have the skills to achieve it.

Do you notice the difference? The second sentence appeals to something Albert Bandura (from chapter three) calls the belief in self-efficacy. The women from the Konstanz mathematics study used the same model. The internal picture of having what it takes to manage problems awakens much hidden potential. For example, 53 percent for a math test ...

That our »potential« also repeatedly surprises us was proven in 1995 by Dov Eden and Yaakov Zuk from Tel Aviv University. Their test subjects were 25 Navy cadets. A common complaint among those venturing into open sea is seasickness. To date, only a few reliable drugs are known. The few that exist – well, most people, out of convenience, take them only when they feel the symptoms of seasickness. However, by this time, it is usually too late, because they are vomiting and unable to keep the remedy in their stomachs.

Eden and Zuk designed a unique experiment for those cadets who had never gone out to sea. Preliminarily, the chosen cadets had to carry out some insignificant tests. A few days later, the scientists randomly selected half the cadets and told them in confidential interviews, »From your test results, we recognise you have a greater ability to handle seasickness than most other people. With your performance, you will surpass most of the other cadets. However, we are asking you not to share this information with any other cadets, so they do not feel demotivated.«

Just like the experiment with the Stanford students and the Konstanz women, the cadets' internal pictures changed and so did their abilities. Their potential unfolded its impact, and they manifested different behaviours. After their first five-day trip out to the ocean, the cadets with the positively altered pictures reported no or little seasickness. The measure of their subjectively perceived symptoms was 42 percent lower than that of the control group. The objective data supported their subjective feelings: On board was an observation team that documented the behaviour of the cadets. However, this team did not know to which of the two groups the cadets belonged. Those participants told beforehand that they would be less seasick and would perform better achieved, by an average of 52 percent, a better rating by the observation team. Observed were activities such as the »effective execution of tasks,« »social involvement with the crew«, and »visible interest in the ship and its technical systems.«

Johammer | Overwhelmed with confidence

»I believe it pays off often for a company if you put the development of your staff at the epicentre,« says Johann Hammerschmid. The 54-year-old electrical engineer is the founder and co-partner of Hammerschmid Maschinenbau (mechanical engineering) GmbH from the upper Austrian municipality of Bad Leonfelden, near Linz. »Unfortunately, a lot of managers do not see the hidden potential in many of their employees – and even less the economic potential which comes with it.«

I learned of Hammerschmid Maschinenbau through the Austrian writer and filmmaker Johanna Tschautscher. She made a documentary about the enterprise and came across an exceptionally human-centred culture. Because she knew of our culture change initiative, she contacted me. »The culture of open communication, tolerance for mistakes, and learning through confidence fascinates even highly qualified employees. Many have started in this small company, instead of going to the large industrial city of Linz,« Tschautscher wrote. Several months and several phone calls later, I went to Upper Austria for a few days to examine the mechanical engineering company in greater detail.

The core business of Hammerschmid Maschinenbau is the production of specially designed machines for industrial customers. This might be an air suspension for the Mercedes-Benz S-Class or cross-country and jumping skis. If a water faucet manufacturer gets the idea to build something exceptional, he would call the developers in Bad Leonfelden, and so would the food manufacturer that wants a machine that can produce Toast Hawaii automatically.

Johann Hammerschmid was employed in various companies. »Almost always, customers and employees were secondary,« he says. »It was always just about money, never about the people.« Within such a framework he realised, intuitively, he would not find his fortune, so he started his own business in 1995. Only one year later, Hammerschmid added his old business partner, Ludwig Mülleder, and transferred to him 50 percent of his shares. Since then, the two have become inseparable. Mülleder is the critical realist and the necessary corrective to the visionary Hammerschmid. »I still remember how it was when I came to the company, back then,« recalls Martin Reingruber, one of the two current managing executives. »I observed they were dealing with people in a way that was entirely different from what I was used to. It started at school. Mostly, we were shown only what we cannot do. Johann, however, believes people can do a lot more and overwhelms them with confidence. Later, when I climbed the ladder into a leadership position, I realised trust is the only effective way to bring out the best in people.«

Johann Hammerschmid and Ludwig Mülleder handed over the operational business to Martin Reingruber and Edi Jenner after 10 successful years. The »oldies« of the company, however, focused, instead, on an extraordinary project, which became the company's biggest challenge in later years. »There is still one unbroken desire,« Johann Hammerschmid tells me. »The desire to create a product that is good for people but that also generates work and enhances our personal development.« The company fulfilled this wish with its first end-consumer product, the electric motorcycle J1. Mülleder and Hammerschmid located the development, production, and sales of the motorcycle in a subsidiary, Johammer, created especially for this purpose. After some time of playful research, the idea matured in 2009 to the actual product. Back then, electric motorcycles were discussed on the market with a range of 100 kilometres. The Johammer team set its goal at 200 kilometres. It should be a »cruiser« – a motorcycle type that originated in the 90s. Characteristic of this type of electric bike is a long wheelbase, wide handlebars, and a mostly upright sitting position. In addition, the team wanted to create a maintenance-free and recyclable product:

a bold aim for a company that had never built a complete motorised vehicle before. Yet now, they broke new ground. »We acted like children, but with some considerable expertise,« Johann Hammerschmid recalls.

»Design and construction of the J1 differed substantially from standard motorcycles,« says designer Georg Hochreiter. »The external vehicle builder, whom we kept asking for advice, could not always help us. We might as well have approached them with an airplane.« The team was left to itself. Either the external suppliers did not have matching components, or they were too heavy to achieve the desired range of 200 kilometres. The staff was gathering a lot of knowledge about the previously unknown area of vehicle manufacturing. Many components had to be developed from scratch. »What the team developed and achieved during this time moved me deeply,« says Johann Hammerschmid. »They released unbelievable potential.«

An essential element for the results of the developer was the internal attitude Johann Hammerschmid showed. The term coined by Reingruber – »overwhelmed us with confidence« – was ubiquitous. And it had an impact. »Johanns' faith in me and in the idea that, eventually, we would find a solution influenced me so much that I ended up believing it myself,« says George Hochreiter.

Initially, the Johammer team set out on a particular body construction, even if they had to buy the required machinery for 100,000 euro. »However, after extensive research, we could build it ourselves for only 20,000 euro,« says Hochreiter. »Eventually, we came up with an entirely different, yet simpler solution. This allowed us to save more time and money.«

Even regarding the steering, the team had to re-think the concept, and it constructed something that had never been done before. »We transferred the way of driving a car to a motorcycle,« says Hochreiter. »It couldn't be any different with the J1 design. The J1 has an unusual appearance, which reminds [one] of a mix of foliage beetles and an insect with long antennae. In this way, the laws of physics prevent steering as it is known from bicycles or motorcycles.

»If we used ›typical‹ standard components, we would never have achieved the minimum quantities,« Hochreiter recalls. »Currently, we are planning to manufacture a few hundred J1. However, for suppliers, we are only interesting if we would buy 20,000 components.« Therefore,

Johammer had to come up with the strategy of making almost all their needed components themselves.

Yet, it was not only the suppliers who gave them a hard time, nor did they even receive possible state funding for sustainable product development – the jury did not believe in Johammer and the J1. It would take several years before the company from Bad Leonfelden received the prestigious Innovation Award of the Wuerzburg Automotive Summit. Reingruber reflects: »Through the trust and faith we received from Hans and Ludwig, most of us unconsciously developed higher confidence in the team. Many of my colleagues have lots of trust in each other by now.« Johann Hammerschmid made sure people, not economic indicators, were in the foreground.

Company: Hammerschmid Maschinenbau GmbH
Industry: Special purpose machinery manufacturer
Headquarters: Bad Leonfelden, Austria
Established: 1996
Employees: 40
Website: www.hammerschmid-mb.com, www.johammer.com
Noteworthy: Without external financing this small company developed – with a high amount of trust in its employees – an Electric Motorcycle. In many aspects, this motorbike outmatches the technical details of big brands.

While I visited the company, some employees told me they had the impression that the J1 was invented only for the employees to grow beyond themselves. Johann Hammerschmid nourished this suspicion when he told me: »In fact, we are a large factory for personality development.« Even though the economic factor takes a backseat, it is working: The entire Johammer project has been financed from its cash flow for years now.

One of the biggest technical challenges was the battery system of Johammer. »If we had chosen just the products available on the market, we would have reached only 50 percent of the range,« says Reingruber. »Either they did not have enough capacity or they were too big and too heavy.« As always, Johann Hammerschmid believed in his team. The battery system is now one of the masterpieces of Johammer. The engineers decided –

without knowing it – on the same building blocks as the car manufacturer Tesla Motors, a pioneer of the electric car industry. »That was in 2010,« says Martin Reingruber. »At that time, Tesla Motors was still in internal development and had not yet offered its battery systems to the market. Even today, Tesla sells its batteries only for the Electro-Smart and the B-Class of Mercedes. We would not be able to purchase their systems.«

The Johammer team, therefore, went with the proven concept of »build it yourself« and ultimately, was very successful. The developers came up with an ingenious idea: a battery system that can consist of more than 1,000 individual cells, held together by a mechanical framework. A second electronic framework connects the cells to each other, so the electricity can flow between them. The developers of the J1 thought, »Two frameworks consume more space and are heavier than one framework.« With the firm belief of their boss, they started fiddling and actually developed a revolutionary battery system that requires only one framework that takes on both the mechanical and the electronic tasks. »It was a tribute to us when the Japanese team of Panasonic came to us and looked at our little factory,« says Martin Reingruber. »The fundamental building block of our battery systems is a lithium-ion cell by Panasonic. That meant we had to win their trust. Only then did Panasonic begin to supply us with large amounts of battery cells. By now, we are providing a handful of other companies with our final battery system,« said Reingruber, pleased. Johammer guarantees the batteries of the J1 will last for 200,000 kilometres. Then the batteries start their second life, so to speak. They can be installed in the solar power system of a house and serve there as a means of energy storage for many years to come.

The strategy of unfolding potential at Hammerschmid and Johammer does not end at the core business, the design of machines. In 2003, the company had already developed so much they also had to expand spatially. »We could have stayed small; however, eventually, we would have become uninteresting for our employees,« Johann Hammerschmid recalls. »Yet, we didn't want to build something that would not represent the way we think.« Because they found no vendors who offered a production hall or who could make one to suit Hammerschmid's needs, there was just one solution: Do it yourself. Eventually, Mülleder and Hammerschmid found a wood builder similarly used to thinking outside of the box. Without further ado, they hired him from another company and let him get accustomed. For several months, the new employee listened to the company and soon understood what made the staff and executives tick. After that, Johann Hammerschmid let him get started. »We still needed an external architect, but for construction technology, I let the new employee just do his thing.« The wood builder began to fiddle and, finally, created a 1,300-square-meter hall for half of the market cost. The big surprise came in the winter: The energy consumption of the hall was not more than that of a family home. »In the first year, the heating costs for the 1300-square-meter hall were 1,800 euro,« says Johann Hammerschmid in a pleased way. The woodbuilder had come up with an insulation that proved to be unbeatable. »For example, if in winter the heating breaks down, we notice it only after three days,« an employee told me. »Only then does it get a little chilly in the hall.«

Meanwhile, the first finished J1 were delivered to customers. Even the media responded favourably to the electric motorcycle. Only the exceptional design seems to look a bit odd for some: Enthusiasts of the more traditional design language still have a somewhat difficult time. Many others, however, love the different approach. »With the J1, we finally have a product we can show off, that we can identify with, and that makes us proud,« an employee told me at the end of my multi-day stay in Bad Leonfelden.

»The overall design of the J1, ultimately, cost us only a fraction of what is normal in the industry. I am sure any other manufacturers would have to invest tenfold in a product like the J1,« Johann Hammerschmid says, pleased. »I always knew the guys could do it.«

The attitude of the boss is what ultimately counts

Your personal attitude can hardly be overestimated for influencing the potential of your employees. In 1965, two psychologists, Robert Rosenthal and Lenore Jacobson, demonstrated this effect in a highly regarded experiment. The two scientists conducted intelligence tests in several US elementary schools. They randomly chose 20 percent of the pupils. To the teachers, they stated the unsubstantiated claim those students were on the verge of a leap forward in the following school year. Rosenthal and Jacobson wanted to research what effects the attitude and expectations of the teacher would have on the pupils.

After a year, the scientists could demonstrate that the selected 20 percent experienced tremendous development. After 12 months, almost half of them received, in the same intelligence tests, 20 points more than they had the previous year, reaching growth distinctly higher than the remaining 80 percent of the students. Just the fact that the teachers had positive internal pictures of those pupils led to the fact that the teachers, mostly unconsciously, treated them differently from the rest of the class. Perhaps, they interpreted a wrong answer in a favourable manner; maybe they gave the students a benevolent smile or showed them more attention. As Rosenthal and Jacobson did not observe the classes, they could not see the actual behaviour of the teacher. However, they could prove that the faith of the teacher in the ability of his pupils influenced the pupils' belief in themselves, changing their internal pictures. These students received more access to their dormant potential and, therefore, performed better.

Johann Hammerschmid, too, holds very benevolent and favourable pictures of his employees. He wonders about the bosses of other companies when he says, »Many executives do not see the hidden power inherent in their employees.« With his attitude, he unfolded a lot of previously unused potential within the employees of his company. The result: Exceptional performance. Employee Georg Hochreiter described his inner development to me as follows: »Johann trusted me and gave me responsibility. It was as if my engine was switched on.«

Faith and the amygdala

If, as a manager, you believe in your employees, you influence neural activities within them, particularly in challenging situations. Your belief in them will reduce the activity of the amygdala, and thus gives your employees more access to their mental abilities. The amygdala plays a central role in our anxiety system. You could also call it your »danger detector.« Whenever you are exposed to a real or even perceived danger, your amygdala becomes active. If a motorcycle comes speeding towards you, it is your amygdala that ensures you jump out of the way. If you are out for a walk and you meet a dangerous dog, you freeze. Before your conscious mind has even perceived the motorcycle or the dangerous dog, your amygdala has taken control of your body.

Charles Darwin, the great man who developed the theory of evolution, described in a published essay in 1899 »the expression of emotions in man and animals« when he experienced the force and speed of the activity of the amygdala. Darwin was in a zoo when he put his face against the glass enclosure of a puff adder. Those snakes have a venom supply that could easily kill five people. Darwin wanted to prove his willpower over his instinct by the firm intention not to move when the snake came after him. He knew quite well that the glass panel would protect him from the deadly bite. However, when the snake attacked, Darwin's instincts took over. His sensory organs, like those in other people, sent the information to the amygdala before they arrived in the cerebrum. The amygdala assessed that attack as a threat and had Darwin jump back. He wrote, »As soon as it (the snake) struck my intention was broken. With surprising high speed, I jumped back – and my willpower no longer showed any effect.«

Survival is the core instinct within every human being. It is deeply rooted in our neural networks. The amygdala is the force that fulfils this instinct, even if – as in Darwin's case – there is no real danger. Transferred to our working life, the amygdala responds to perceived fears, even when there is no real threat to our bodies or lives. For some people, the amygdala becomes active when the company announces another change project or a reorganisation process. For others, it might be a new colleague joining the department, who might endanger their job. For me, it was when my boss told me I was to give a presentation at the most prominent meeting of the company. We see danger where there is none. Once our amygdala is active, it not only ensures, through a cascading process, that our adrenal glands secrete stress hormones and change blood pressure and pulse, it also reduces access to the sensitive neural networks in our prefrontal cortex: the place where all of our higher mental achievements and our potential are located. In such (fearful) moments, we no longer have access to everything that lies within us. We are no longer the best version of who we might be. However, dangers recognised by our amygdala are often only perceived threats. It is not the reality, but how we interpret this reality, which leads to the increased activity of the amygdala and all the other stress reactions that come with it. In his Enchiridion of Epictetus, the ancient philosopher Epictetus wrote in 125 AD: »Not things themselves, but the opinions about the same are what disturbs people.«

In 2002, the Stanford researcher Kevin Ochsner and his colleagues from the Massachusetts Institute of Technology put Epictetus' statement to the neuroscience test. The research team proved we are able to reduce the amygdala activity by changing our opinions. A quieter amygdala allows us to regain more access to our prefrontal cortex and its hidden potential. Once again, we can grow beyond ourselves. The amygdala always responds faster than our mind – as in Darwin's case – to protect us from immediate danger. However, within a few moments, consciously directed thoughts can regain control and, therefore, reduce amygdala activity and all its related stress reactions.

Ochsner and his colleagues, in their experiments, determined that the new interpretation of a situation is one of the most efficient ways to achieve this goal. The scientists examined the effect of emotionally disturbing images on the human brain. They showed test participants a photo of crying people in front of a church; the people looked like mourners. Participants were asked to find a more comforting interpretation of this image. In other words, they stayed in touch with the stimuli of the photo, but gave it a new meaning. With the crying people in front of the church, a possible new interpretation could be that they were guests of a wedding party.

The participants could not look away from their photo, nor were they allowed to drift away mentally. All they could do was engage actively with the photo. With some of the unpleasant images, participants were asked simply to look at them and let them sink in. In those cases, the brain scanner in which the test subjects were situated showed heightened activity in the amygdala. With other photos, however, when the participants tried to give the pictures a positive meaning, the brain scanner showed activity in the lateral and medial regions of the prefrontal cortex: The mind was working on the new interpretation. The researchers could immediately observe how, initially, the heightened activity of the amygdala slowed down. Giving the photos a new meaning measurably calmed the neural networks. Inspired by these results, the neuroscientists began the evaluation of their study with Hamlet's phrase:

> »There is nothing either good or bad but thinking makes it so.«
> This is Epictetus' knowledge in Shakespeare's words. Modern
> brain research with the latest technology proves old knowledge!

The reappraisal of a situation can take place only in the brain of the person concerned. Small children, however, are an exception. Observe a child who falls down: First, it glances at Mum. Her reaction will determine whether the child gets up and keeps playing or breaks out in tears. At this young age, the evaluation is still externalised. In adults – for instance, your employees – this externalisation no longer occurs. However, as an executive, you can give impulses for a reappraisal. Once again, look at the Circle of Potential: Experiences influence internal pictures.

If you believe in your employees, you are altering their internal pictures. This is advisable in two situations.

1. Your employees lack reference experiences: When people lack reference experiences, most likely, they are also missing matching internal pictures. Remember when I asked you to imagine writing your name with your dominant hand. After that, I asked you, in your mind, to write your name with the other hand. Most likely, that was much harder for you. The reason: Rarely are you writing with your non-dominant hand; therefore, you are missing the internal pictures. Having no reference experience – that's what happened at Sony Music when I thought I would fail at the important meeting. At that point, the reappraisal of my boss helped me: »I saw you and got good feedback. I am not worried. I know you're gonna rock it.« My initial mind-movie, with the heightened activity of my amygdala and all the corresponding stress responses, died down. I could access my higher mental faculties again.

2. Your employee has had a negative experience: You will encounter people who have had unfavourable experiences, either before you became their boss (for example, Bettina Cramer, the Upstalsboom employee from chapter 1) or throughout the time you have been their boss. The risk of negative experiences is that people quickly develop limiting internal

pictures. If you, once again, look at the Circle of Potential, you will see limiting internal pictures lead to a limited development of the person's potential. Subsequently, those people present only their limited version of themselves, not what they could be. For example, for many years, I held the internal picture that my voice sounded unpleasant. The negative experience that led to this belief was ridiculously insignificant: Some time, back in the 80s, I heard myself on an answering machine. Back then, the recordings were very distorted, and it really didn't sound great. However, 15 years later, at the birthday party of one of my friends in Zurich, I was talking to a radio host about my experience. This man offered me a reassessment by credibly assuring me that my voice sounded pleasant. It was because of him that my limiting pictures changed. Without this new evaluation, I don't think I would have ever set foot on a stage, let alone talked in front of audiences of tens of thousands of people every year.

If you see co-workers who have had negative experiences, as a good boss it is your duty, in a professional context, to make sure this does not lead to limiting pictures. We encounter negative experiences constantly. I once was working with the CEO of a DAX enterprise who loved to have his employees ›for breakfast.‹ If he had a bad day, the whole team got to feel it. He even seemed pleased with himself. »People need to learn to stand up to me,« he told me when I confronted him and told him that he caused a lot of anxiety in people. In periodic intervals, each department had to deploy employees to the management meetings to present issues of particular importance. There was a 50:50 chance those employees would get caught on a day when the CEO was in a bad mood.

Getting back to the model of the Circle of Potential: These people had negative experiences. There was the realistic risk they would develop unfavourable pictures. However, this company also had good executives who offered a reappraisal to the affected staff. For example, they would tell the staff that the CEO was known for putting down excellent staff. Or they would point out the great preparation the staff had done for those CEO meetings. There were ongoing discussions with this CEO; however, sometimes reality does not change. In those situations, it might be helpful to remember Epictetus, Shakespeare, or Kevin Ochsner.

Essence for Executives

Trust – People need someone who believes in them

- Successful leaders believe in their employees, strengthening their internal pictures. Stronger internal pictures lead to better unfolding and development of employee potential.
- The trainees of Weleda AG founded their own company, sold their own products and improved trade relations with one of the company's most important customers. Their confidence increased noticeably, because management gave them lots of confidence.
- Participants in one study scored higher by 53 percent in a math problem than the control group. Before the test, they worked for only 3 minutes on their confidence in their capabilities.
- Inner attitude is crucial: An experiment showed the faith of teachers in their students resulted in better marks, compared to the pupils in whom they believed less.
- »Our boss overwhelmed us with confidence and trust.« So said the employees of the mechanical engineer Hammerschmid. As a result, the workforce developed, without external financing, an electric motorbike, which is in many aspects technically superior to the products of other famous companies.
- If people feel that someone believes in them, they will come out on the other side with strength after going through difficult or unknown situations. The confidence of a boss in his staff helps them assess negative experiences differently.

Chapter 5

Experiences – people grow when challenged

»I wish all my colleagues could make the same experience we did.«

Victoria Schwab, student, dm-drugstore chain

»If you have ever been through a 12-hour shootout, then you couldn't care less if the boss, once again, brought the deadline for the latest project forward one week,« a man told me in finest British English.

His words are not a metaphor. Indeed, he had been in a 12-hour shootout in Iraq. Some of his comrades died within a few meters of him, and a bullet grazed his helmet, leaving a lifelong memory of how close he had come to death. »It takes at least a week to regenerate physically,« he says. »During the battle, you are running on adrenaline for hours – for days to come, my kidneys were sore.« Whenever he talks about his engagement in combat, he refers to himself as »you« and never as »I.«

I met men like him often during the years I lived in Zurich: former British soldiers, who are now working in the private sector, and due to good job offers, came to Switzerland. Some of the older ones were sent to the Falklands War by Margaret Thatcher, while some of the younger ones were sent to Iraq by Tony Blair. What seems to unite them all: Compared to their non-veteran colleagues, they seem to have higher stress resistance. Due to the existential threat they all had lived through, these people can better put stressful situations and power games into perspective within the context of a company. Stress, to them, has a different meaning.

Perhaps, you know it from your professional life: If it gets dicey, one gets some older colleagues on board, not just because of their knowledge, but also because those people are much more likely to deal with those difficult situations more calmly. A few years ago, the ING-bank initiated a training program explicitly for people aged 50 and older. The executives observed that those people, due to their many years of experience, can deal with situations in a much more relaxed manner and could come up with more solutions, which could enrich younger teams, a project leader told me.

That people grow and mature with experience is an axiom. Yet, many executives leave this potential unexploited, mostly because they do not know about the underlying pattern. There are other companies that create specific areas of experience, so those people can develop their potential. This benefits not only the individual, but the whole company: They are employing people who deliver clearly better results than some of their competitors.

dm | Learning on the job

»I have a feeling that something special is lived within our company,« says the young woman with a red coat. »Here, you can immediately experience how the role of a company can change society.« It is November 2012. I had given a lecture at Alanus University of Bonn and was leading students and company representatives through a reflection workshop, when I caught this sentence from a workgroup. Intrigued, I participated in the conversation of the attendees. Student Victoria Schwab, who coined this term, does her internship at the drugstore chain »dm«, where she takes part in a multi-award-winning training concept. »It is self-evident that the company, and our work, are part of our lives,« she says. »It is very important you see yourself as a human being with an individual personality and to engage yourself as such.«

In 2012, in an employee opinion survey carried out at its headquarters in Karlsruhe, 98 percent of employees stated they would recommend dm as an employer. Throughout Europe, dm employs 55,000 people in more than 3,200 stores and has achieved a turnover of 9 billion euro. »For us, the sales are not a business goal,« says Managing Director for Human Resources Christian Harms. »A high turnover, for us, is the result of customers' and employees' satisfaction.« This first, and so far last, survey led to a surprise among the pollsters: The five lowest-rated criteria still received such a good rating that, in other companies, they would have made it into the top five.

It was the new millennium that marked a change for dm. The company grew rapidly. That was one reason the management level revised its apprenticeship concept. »By today, we train three times as many people – for economic reasons, as well,« says Christian Harms. However, the really remarkable change took place in its conduct and content. »This was, in no way, economically driven, quite the contrary.« The newly developed training concept of the drugstore chain was based on the fact that the trainees should get as many different experiences as possible. The company believed that, with this concept, the trainees would develop better and more sustainable potential than with conventional training methods. An internal guide for the trainers states this clearly: »Practice is more important than theory.« The two applications in which the dm experimental approach puts this successfully into reality are called »LidA (Lernen in der Arbeit = Learning on the job)« and »Adventure of Culture.«

»For every question I asked, I got a question back,« Victoria Schwab says about her education. »The expectation is, first ask yourself and try to find your own way.« Schwab alternates with one semester at Alanus University and the other semester at her internship with other »learners« at dm. The word »learner« (rather than »apprentice«) expresses a special attitude, which embodies the education concept at dm. »You can't instruct anyone,« says Christian Harms. »Neither can you motivate someone. Some things can come only from within the person. We wish for our students to take an active role during the training. We want them to learn, rather than to be taught.«

This change of name also changed the role of the instructors and trainees. From then on, dm was no longer looking for trainers with purely technical expertise, but instead began to educate so-called learning companions for their learners. These companions acquired the expertise to lead the learners from one learning experience to the next skilfully.

The LidA concept is based on the old Confucian wisdom: »Tell me and I will forget. Show me and I will remember. Let me do it and I will understand.«

»The idea of learning by doing it is nothing new,« Christian Harms states. »Everyone who gets a new car or even a television set has the same experience. However, to systematise this concept, we had to develop a new approach to learning. We recruited external help.«

From the very first day of his or her training at dm, every trainee gets special preparation for his or her education. In so-called »LidA-work-days,« the newbie learns all about the training concept. How does LidA work? Why is it dm's chosen training concept? What is expected of the learner? »Most of our trainees know what to expect before the start of their training,« says Agnes Allinger, Area Manager for Employee Recruitment and Media. »We offer open days where young people can come and spend one day with us. At this point, they are treated like learners and, therefore, can experience first-hand what this self-discovery learning concept feels like.«

Company: dm-Drogerie Markt GmbH + Co. KG
Industry: Health Trade and Manufacturing
Headquarters: Karlsruhe, Germany
Established: 1973
Employees: 55,000
Website: www.dm.de
Noteworthy: The trainees of the company receive a high degree of autonomy through a special training concept, called LidA (Lernen in der Arbeit = learning on the job).

In addition, the students participated in two theatre workshops, where they make experiences far beyond their everyday working life. This experience helps them to significantly increase confidence when dealing with customers.

Once the LidA-training begins, the instructor creates the framework and tasks. After that, it is up to the learners to determine how to reach the goal. To find answers to their tasks, the students have different media available, such as the intranet, newsletters, or product flyers. »In the early days of LidA, we informed the trainers about all details, but not the other branch employees,« says Christian Harms. »Back then, the learners would just go to one of their store colleagues and ask for the solution. However, by now, the LidA training concept is established in all branches and departments. All colleagues now know the learners must make their own experiences to develop the best way possible.«

»For example, if we are planning a promotion for baby food in one of our departments, we ask the trainees how they would go about doing that,« says Manuela Franz, advisor for education and training. »And then, we leave the planning and implementation completely to the trainee. We firmly believe the solutions the students find for themselves are much more likely to be remembered than solutions given to them.« Moreover, it seems the trainees often come up with better solutions than the trainer had in mind. The trainees I met in the departments confirm this impression. »In the meantime, I have worked in three departments and experienced that the same task was tackled differently each time,« trainee Felix Woller told me. »Again and again, I realised how much freedom we have in our training.«

If you engage in a training concept, based to a high degree on trainees' own experiences, you have to realise that plenty of mistakes will be made. »This is, for the trainees, a major challenge,« says training consultant Manuela Franz. »Many of the young people experience a mistake as a personal failure. It's normal that, sometimes, things go wrong. That is the best way to remember to do it differently the next time.« dm takes worry about errors seriously. In the LidA manual for instructors, you will find a whole chapter devoted to the culture of error. The trainers are instructed to encourage students to be consciously aware of their errors, to address them, and then reflect on them. Reflection is an important part of LidA. dm holds the opinion that any experience is strengthened only when it is discussed in its context. This kind of training requires an internal clear orientation and lots of discipline. »Only since I have been working with the young learners have I realised how difficult it has to be for the instructors,« Viktoria Schwab remembers. »We all have the impulse to help. You always have to step back to let them find their own way and not hand them the solution.«

The highlight of the LidA-training will be experienced by the young people in their final year. Throughout Germany, about 30 dm drugstores will become so-called »learnerstores« for several weeks. The permanent staff makes room for the young people and works at sister stores for four to six weeks. During this time, the entire store is handed over to the learners. The average age of the staff in these drugstores abruptly changes to the early 20s. During those six weeks, there are neither trainers nor other executives on site. The young people are fully responsible.

»I was in the role of the branch manager last week,« reported learner Rita Green of her experience in a Hanover branch. »In the beginning, I was worried my learner colleagues would not take me seriously in this role. My fear was unfounded. Most impressive for me was that I was allowed to participate at a regional branch manager meeting with 14 other ›real‹ store managers.« Laughing, she adds, »Nevertheless, my work is relaxed again, since a different trainee took on the role of the store manager after me.« To prepare for this deployment, the young trainees met for a two-day workshop. They chose a branch manager and a deputy for each of the forthcoming four weeks. They also agreed on their own rules as to how they would cooperate with each other, and they created deployment plans. »We agreed the word of the store manager is not set in stone,« learner Felix Woller told me. »Over the past two years, we had already learned to think independently.«

dm | The Adventure of Culture

»Some of us grew far beyond ourselves,« Felix Woller told me. He is in his second year and has already experienced the »Adventure of Culture.« His trainee colleague, Rita Green, has experienced it twice. »The first time, I thought this was terrible. The second time, however, it was better. In retrospect, I became a lot more confident.«

Christian Harms, managing director for HR, knows this phenomenon. »Initially, with LidA, we experienced resistance among colleagues in the store. We often had to explain why we train differently now. However, with the ›Adventure of Culture‹, we experienced resistance among the learners at the beginning. ›I am not here to act in a puppet theatre‹ was the first reaction in 2002/2003. In the meantime, however, thousands of learners are telling us that, at the end of their training, this part was among the best of their entire time.«

Adventure of Culture consists of two intensive theatre workshops in the first and second year. The company created a situation in which the young learners could have experiences, which they would not have any other way. Now, dm employs 170 actors, directors, and theatre educators each season, who guide the young people through these workshops. Within six to eight weeks, the trainees meet for eight long days. There, they discuss a common play, roles are assumed, and the entire set is created, including the sewing of the costumes. Of course, they also rehearse. Some groups are based on classics, like Shakespeare's »Romeo and Juliet« or Horváth's »Faith, Love, Hope.« Other workshops address a more personal concern, such as how we deal with time or youth violence.

»It is our conscious decision that the trainees do not just re-enact any work situations,« says Christian Harms. »The theatre workshops are supposed to be separate from their training period in the stores.« When I spoke to Viktoria Schwab again, she was right in the middle of the Adventure of Culture. »For the first time, we had a crisis yesterday. We asked ourselves why we were actually playing the piece we had rehearsed all the time. However, that is not all that bad if you realise that crises are normal and helpful to get on with the process.«

»The greatest benefit is the confident appearance and improved communication among them,« confirmed trainee Johannes Schmitt. »The shyer among us have learned not to fear the dominant learners. We all have learned that a lot can change when listening to the quiet people.«

During their theatre workshops, the trainees have no contact with their dm colleagues. These workshops are conducted entirely by externally employed artists. Karsten Röth is the exception; he is one of five dm sponsors, who takes care of the Adventure of Culture.

»Adventure of Culture is a space free of evaluations,« says Röth. »Interestingly, this creates a lot of stress among the trainees. From school they are used to being evaluated rather quickly. They have high standards for themselves. In the beginning, it is unsettling for the young people not to know where they stand.« Those theatre workshops are not individual sessions, but a group process. To see what you can put together is a meaningful experience for the young people, regarding how to collaborate within a team. Later in life, this can be very valuable.

The grand finale of each workshop is performing the play in front of an audience. The trainees invite family, friends, and colleagues from the stores. The experience of the workshops, followed by the public performance, changes the trainees. If they can stand on stage in front of hundreds of people, the hurdle of approaching a customer suddenly becomes insignificant. »Sometimes, these transformations can be seen at the performances,« says Manuela Franz. »Suddenly, a very, very quiet trainee is on stage and plays an extroverted supporting role. For many, this development continues throughout the rest of their traineeship. The experience that ›I have mastered something I did not believe I was able to do‹ is very formative.« A branch manager, who as a former learner had been on stage herself adds: »I am always moved to tears to see what those young people are capable of today.«

The Adventure of Culture was implemented simultaneously with the LidA learning concept at the turn of the millennium. Entrepreneur Götz Werner got his inspiration for the Adventure of Culture from a book by Rainer Patzlaff entitled »Kindheit verstummt« (»Silenced Childhood«). »Back then, health insurance studies showed quite clearly the consequences for children who consume more electronic media, while at the same time, having less contact with real people,« says Christian Harms. »The German health insurance company AOK calculated that the cost of speech therapists won't be affordable in the long run. The day young people no longer have the courage to approach customers – this, for us, as a trading business with lots of stores, would be a disaster.«

dm tested several pilot projects: a course in visual arts, a video project, and a theatre workshop. »The biggest changes could be seen in those people who participated in the theatre workshops. We also have a social responsibility,« says Christian Harms. »Therefore, we had to begin to work differently with our learners.«

When I spoke to Victoria Schwab, the student from Alanus, for the last time in 2014, she had just finished her internship at dm. »During the Adventure of Culture, when we changed from content to the more personal level, the unity between us had changed dramatically,« she recalls. »Through this experience, real development has taken place. I would hope we learners are not the only ones with this experience, but all of my colleagues in dm, as well.«

What exactly happened with the learners, who could interact differently with customers after attending the theatre workshops? How did the LidA training change these young people? What patterns do these two formative experiences, which dm provides to its trainees each year, follow?

The Circle of Potential helps one comprehend the impact of experiences in developing human potential. Let me start with a personal experience. Many years ago, when I went to school in my hometown, Brunswick, during a rather memorable year, I received a »failed« for the first time: in English. In the natural sciences, I was between »very good« and »good«, due to a very good teacher. My internal pictures were something like: »Well, languages are just not my thing.« I put biology and chemistry in my advanced courses, succeeded, and so prepared myself for my medical studies. For many years to come, I was convinced that English and I had to go our separate ways. Those earlier negative experiences shaped my internal pictures of myself and my abilities.

Throughout a lifetime, many people have negative experiences: Some are abandoned by their partner. Others are yelled at by the boss or do not get the attention they want from a person important to them. If you read autobiographies of famous people, you often find they were shaped by a difficult, often even missing, parent. The list of possible negative experiences is long and diverse. They are normal and part of life so we can grow.

The risk of negative experiences you know from the previous chapter: Automatically, sometimes unconsciously, people develop limiting internal pictures. As a result, they live only a fraction of their potential. One could intervene at the level of internal pictures – for example, by offering a re-evaluation, as you came to know in the last chapter. If a good friend is left by her partner, people will tell her she will soon find someone better. If the boss has yelled at your colleague, you tell him in a believable manner that he has done a good job.

However, the magic bullet to invalidate negative experiences (so that no limiting internal pictures can be created) is something else: You must solve the problem at the level of the Circle of Potential, where it was created. If you have fallen off the horse, encouragement and the trust

of your instructor help. However, to »cure« the negative experience, you have to get right back on the horse and replace the negative with a positive experience.

Just to stay with this metaphor – I did not get back on the horse again for many years after I had failed English at school. Only after I had started my job at Sony Music, where I had to liaise with European superiors in London and the headquarters in New York, did I venture back to the English language. This time, I had new, more supportive experiences.

Gerald Hüther likes to tell a story in a different context that fits here well: If a 75-year-old man goes to community college to learn Chinese, this is a lengthy and cumbersome process. However, were the same man to fall in love with a Chinese woman and move with her to a Chinese province, he would learn the language much more effortlessly and quickly. This happened to me when I worked »in the new world« of Sony Music. Soon, English and I were good friends. After a few years, I moved to the Swedish communications equipment supplier Ericsson and took an internationally leading position. Ninety percent of my daily communication was held in English. Whether e-mails, phone calls, global strategy papers, contracts, or corporate policy work with the European Commission, I always excelled it. With these new positive experiences, my internal pictures about my abilities changed. Looking at the model of the Circle of Potential, I could increase access to my potential and, therefore, change my behaviour. What this means, in reality, is that my foreign language skills took a quantum leap! By now, some of my clients who have heard me lecture in German and in English tell me I seem more relaxed and that I get to the point more quickly when I speak English.

A »failed« in English at school ... had life not given me a second chance – a better experience – I would still bear the limiting internal picture: »Languages are just not my thing.«

We are all influenced by big and small negative experiences. And it's the negative situations that leave an imprint, rather than the positive ones. Our brains are designed this way so that we protect ourselves in the future. »That was just when I remembered to do it differently the next time,« explains dm Training Consultant Manuela Franz. That is the reason errors in their training are downright desirable. dm ensures trainees consciously reflect on their mistakes. If this reflection does not take place, the error »embeds« as a negative experience and unconsciously creates limiting internal pictures. I experienced, even among very successful, brilliant, and accomplished executives, that actions were limited by such old internal pictures. They often report a vague feeling or behaviour they cannot explain. If, in a coaching session, we dig a little deeper, often long-forgotten experiences surface. Usually, they are met with a sentence, such as: »I would never have thought that this is still influencing me.« During such a session, I use this access to their internal pictures to dissolve the blockages.

You can safely assume this is the same for a considerable part of your team. Those people, too, hold limiting internal pictures. Would it not be like that, they would bristle with self-confidence, and they would be free of any internal and interpersonal conflicts. The good news: Limiting internal pictures created by negative experiences can be changed. An effective way is new, positive experiences through which people can grow.

The experiences of the dm learners reveal wonderfully how behaviour can be changed with more access to a person's potential.

1. To speak during the theatre workshops to a large crowd of people led to a different behaviour while dealing with customers in their daily work. »The biggest benefit is the confident appearance,« trainee John Schmitt recalls.

2. The experience of crisis during rehearsals helped develop greater conflict handling ability in the long run. »Especially when we changed from content to the more personal level, the unity between us changed dramatically. Through this experience, real development has taken place,« Viktoria Schwab reflected.

3. Experience of high self-responsibility during the LidA training helped develop behaviour with healthy self-confidence, according to Felix Woller. »We all have learned in the previous years to think independently!«

Experiences shape the young brain

> »In all beginnings dwells a magic force
> For guarding us and helping us to live.«
>
> *from »Stages« by Hermann Hesse*

The »Center for the Developing Child« at Harvard University describes the magic of beginning with a number: 700 new synapses per second. The neural phenomenon of a young person can be described by this number of new nerve cell connections, which emerge in our minds throughout the early years, second by second. Because our brains and genes do not know the context and the conditions under which we are born, we are all presented with an oversupply of synaptic connections, which we develop in the first few months of our lives. The Harvard researchers differentiate this oversupply: Of the 700-per-second emerging neural connections, the majority grow into the sensory networks within the first months. These are the parts of the brain responsible for the perception of the environment through hearing, taste, smell, sight, and touch. At the age of four to five months, the number of synapses reaches its pinnacle in this area of the brain; after that, they start to decrease slowly. However, the networks for the basic understanding of language are hot on their heels. About eight months after birth, you can determine the maximum connection density in the brain area in charge of language skills. Those neural areas, which will be responsible for higher mental capabilities later in life, achieve their lifelong largest connection density about one year after birth. From there, everything slows down – at least as far as the nerve cell synapses are concerned. Two-thirds of the synaptic connections dissolve again.

However, you don't need to worry: Our brains are working with as little effort as possible. That also means connections, which are no longer required, will disappear. »Use it or lose it« is one law of this restructuring. Another law is »neurons which fire together wire together.« The networks commonly used stabilise their connections and grow closer together. This early childhood structuring of the brain – neuroplasticity – takes place rapidly. Unlike in adults, every experience impresses on a child's brain in the form of neural connections. Michael Merzenich, a pioneer of neuro-plasticity, describes it as follows: »The learning machine is switched on permanently.« The brain of a small child cannot distinguish important from unimportant and, therefore, takes in everything. However, if there is a lack of experience, the brain can form only a few new networks.

Former Romanian dictator Nicolae Ceausescu is responsible for the following brutal example. To make the size of his people grow artificially, he issued Decree 770, rendering school sex education, all contraceptives, and abortion criminal acts. It threatened penalties of up to 25 years in prison. Women of childbearing age were systematically monitored to detect early signs of pregnancy. This was followed by the birth of about 2 million so-called Decree children. Over 100,000 of them grew up in crowded and understaffed child facilities. Many were badly neglected. After the Romanian Revolution in 1989, a team of scientists from various Western hospitals and universities was formed under the name »The Bucharest Early Intervention Project.« In an eight-year long-term study, they examined what effect the lack of stimuli, the lack of experience, and the lack of social interaction had had on these children. They managed to find foster homes for some, while others had to remain in the facilities. Using brain scans, the research team could make visible the effects associated with neglect and the lack of early experiences: The brains of the children in the facility homes showed less grey matter. This is the area of the brain that contains the nerve cell bodies. The white matter – the area with the nerve cell synapses – was also smaller than in control groups of children who had grown up in a family from birth.

In a paper published in 2011, the researchers summarised the findings of their study. The most likely explanation for this brain development was the lack of experience, they wrote.

Encouraging, however, was that the volume of white matter – the nerve cell synapses – normalized after a few years for those children placed in foster homes.

The Romanian legacy of children's homes is shocking. Yet, in many families – usually unnoticed – something else takes place worldwide. It is another lack of experience, which leads to a measurable change in a child's brain development: Overprotection. Maybe you can recall someone from your circle of friends or acquaintances who belongs to this species of parents. The first few months, no one but the parents may hold the baby. The risk of an infection is just too high. If you visit this family, you have to whisper, because even after six months, the new-born is still sensitive to noise and, above all, is not to be disturbed in its sleep. Mobiles must always be in airplane mode or switched off, because of the risk of radiation. The food is matched to the blood group or the Five Elements Kitchen – until puberty.

At the Japanese Gunma University, researcher Kosuke Narita and eight of his colleagues of the Department of Psychiatry and Human Behaviour started to investigate the influence of such parents on their children. Previous studies have shown that patients with psychiatric problems, such as schizophrenia, mood disorders, and obsessive-compulsive disorder, most likely were highly under- or overprotected during their childhoods. They had parents who withheld from the child the experience of life. »Current imaging techniques have shown that abnormalities of the left dorsolateral prefrontal cortex (DLPFC) are closely connected with affective disorders, schizophrenia, and regulating emotions,« said the Japanese research team at the beginning of their 2010 published study. The scientists put one and one together. If overprotection may result in certain psychiatric ailments, and if those illnesses can be connected to certain changes in the corresponding part of the brain, it would be worth looking at this part of the brain of overprotected children, even if no mental illness is present.

Therefore, the researchers recruited 50 Japanese individuals, with an average age of 25, and subjected them to a survey and a brain scan. The survey, a Parental Bonding Instrument (PBI), aimed to learn from the young adults how they experienced their upbringing until their 16th birthday. With the brain scanner and functional magnetic resonance imaging, they also looked closely at the left DLPFC of participants. The results of the survey versus the brain scans confirmed the presumption of researchers. »Under- and overprotection appears to trigger morphological abnormalities of the DLPFC,« they summarised in their study.

The Japanese scientists confirmed that a structural change within the brain occurred as a result of neglect, just as it was recognised in the children in the Romanian child facilities. In addition, however, they proved that overprotection, and holding back experiences, also results in structural changes in the brains of children!

The realisation: Our experiences influence the structure of our brain. Especially during our childhood, our brain is highly plastic; almost every experience leads to a corresponding network. However, a lack of experience means that existing neural networks will dissolve.

Upstalsboom | Growth in cascades

»I find it unfortunate that it is already over,« said Thomas Schwertfirm at the beginning of 2015. The 27-year-old student and two fellow students from the Department of Tourism Management at the University of Munich had spent six months in Borkum. The trio had just finished their internship at the Upstalsboom Seehotel. During this time, they not only co-supervised the hotel operationally, but also developed a new strategy, including alterations and related financing. »Now, we are on the verge of the reconstruction to start, but unfortunately, we must go back to university,« Schwertfirm lamented.

The three students experienced the effects of an intervention, which the managing director, Bodo Janssen, had implemented in a very different area. The whole story started a few years earlier with a hotel director in Emden: Dennis Schweikard. »I have been with the company since 1993, and I know by which values the family Janssen works. Otherwise, I probably would not have stayed during 2010/2011,« Schweikard told me. »I was new to my role as a hotel director, and with my direct supervisor, I witnessed something I did not know from Upstalsboom.« Bodo Janssen adds: »I used to think Mr. Schweikard was unproductive as a hotel director and that he basically just did what he was told to do.« Until 2011, there was an additional management level between Janssen and Schweikard. Because Schweikard was not directly reporting to Janssen, the head of the company was not able to pinpoint where exactly the inefficiency could be …

»Back then, I was simply dissatisfied with some of the behaviours of those people who ranked above the hotel directors,« Janssen recalls. »Professionally, they were top quality, but on a human level, they fit less and less with our culture. They did not share the vision of happy people – quite the contrary.« Janssen always sought a dialogue with those two people, but his desire for more humanity towards the hotel directors who were their subordinates, they either could not or would not meet.

At some stage, Janssen simply had enough and gradually got them out the door. »The most amazing thing for me was the development of Mr. Schweikard,« says Janssen. »There was a lot of untapped potential because, in my opinion, he had been deliberately kept down for a long time.«

»During every phone call with the area manager, I feet like I lost a pound in weight,« says Dennis Schweikard. He is still emotional when he thinks back to this time. Schweikard had to sign off on any decision by his superior, even whether a new employee should start one week earlier, he says. »It was common for staff to get me out of internal meetings, because my boss regularly phoned, commanded me to the phone, and I had to stand questions and answer. I felt treated condescendingly.«

Only after Janssen removed this executive-level employee entirely from the company was Schweikard capable of acting freely and how he saw fit, as was commonplace in Upstalsboom. Bodo Janssen gave the hotel director all the freedom he needed; the main thing was that the figures had to be right. Schweikard finally tried himself in his role. »The employee satisfaction in my house went up,« he remembers. »After a few weeks, I received the first positive feedback. Even the feedback from our customers at portals like ›HolidayCheck‹ improved. And ultimately, our revenues went up, too.«

Company: Upstalsboom Hotel + Freizeit GmbH & Co. KG
Industry: Hotels and Holiday Apartments
Headquarters: Emden, Germany
Established: 1970
Employees: 650
Website: www.upstalsboom.de
Noteworthy: Through a so-called happiness-strategy, the employee satisfaction and the revenues doubled within three years. In the last year, the profit margin increased by 40 percent.

Today, Schweikard is one of the most versatile Upstalsboom directors. »He has achieved an increase in earnings of 30 percent now that he has the framework he needs,« says Janssen. »Above all, he managed to create a similar environment for other people, as well, so they could make new experiences and grow beyond themselves.«

An example of Schweikard's successful leadership is Yvonne Klein. The student wrote her bachelor's thesis on Upstalsboom and later applied for an internship. However, instead of an internship, she received a hotel. »We had closed the Seehotel on Borkum, since it no longer matched our group and was economically unattractive,« says Janssen. »I offered Mrs. Klein the chance to reopen and manage this hotel.«

Dennis Schweikard took on the role of mentor for Yvonne Klein. The student spent one week in his Emden hotel to learn, side by side with Dennis Schweikard, the processes at Upstalsboom. Then, she went to Borkum. Two weeks later, Klein received her first guests in the reopened Seehotel.

»Mr. Schweikard did not order me to do anything,« the 29-year-old recalls about her sponsor. »Previously, I had experienced things differently. During my studies, I worked in several hotels. Everywhere, there were clear rules and guidelines. When I introduced a new idea, the answer usually was, ›We've always done it that way.‹ My sponsor, Mr. Schweikard, actually invited me to contribute new ideas. If I had any questions or problems, I called him. Instead of giving me solutions, he first listened to my ideas. There was great trust between us.«

Since spring 2013, the young woman has been managing her own hotel. »From Munich to Borkum was an unexpected and big step,« she says. »But my partner, too, thought this offer was very unique. I just had to accept it, even though it meant a long-distance relationship for us. Such an opportunity rarely comes in life.«

Dennis Schweikard and Bodo Janssen met upfront. Together, they tried to figure out how to reopen the Seehotel with the least possible effort. »In the past, it was a hotel and restaurant. That meant a lot of personnel,« Janssen recalls. »We decided to reduce the offer to a bed and breakfast.« The cleaning of the 39 rooms was taken over by an external service provider. The internal staff consisted of five employees. »Ms. Klein has a quality I would wish from every employee: She has the courage to acknowledge to herself what she can and what she can't do,« says Bodo Janssen. »She sees the support of her sponsor as appreciation. This is not always self-evident: Especially with us in the hotel business, support is often perceived as re-delegation or a lack of confidence in the performance of individuals. This, too, is an experience that many of us have yet to make: Some things can be achieved only within the community.«

If she is not taking care of guests or managing the operation, you might see the student going to the hardware store: The small Borkum Hotel is missing a caretaker. She buys the material and then climbs on the roof and performs minor repairs. »If it gets tight at breakfast, she helps with cleaning the tables or washing the dishes in the kitchen,« says Schweikard. »This is a quality you do not often experience in people in her position.«

Meanwhile, Yvonne Klein's third season has begun. During the winter, the hotel is closed. If she is not home in Bavaria to enjoy her holiday, she shadows at headquarters or in other hotels of the Upstalsboom group to get new ideas for her house on Borkum. The relationship between her mentor and the former student has changed over the course of three years. »The mentorship has become a team at par,« says Schweikard. »There are now matters about which I call Ms. Klein to ask for her opinion. In recent years, I perceived her as very inquisitive. Today, she stands with her hotel at an economic breakthrough: She can now expand.«

»I have become much more relaxed,« the young hotel director reflects. »In the early days, I often made myself crazy. By experience, I can now appreciate things much better.«

After Bodo Janssen watched the student for one season, he came up with a new idea. In 2013, the first year the hotel was under the management of Yvonne Klein, she achieved a booking rate of 80 percent. That was the best booking rate in the entire history of the house. That led Janssen to another idea: »What if Ms. Klein passed on her knowledge of growing beyond oneself?« Janssen called the Faculty of Tourism at the University of Munich, where Yvonne Klein studied. Janssen proposed a long-term cooperation. Now, each season, up to three students can do their internship in Borkum under the supervision of Ms. Klein. In spring 2014, Maralen Schiessl, Jonas Fröhlich, and Thomas Schwertfirm made their way to the small North Sea island, northwest of Emden. »Actually, we wanted to come even earlier,« says Thomas Schwertfirm. »We had already received information about the hotel, and we did a lot of thinking about how we could tackle everything.«

In the previous season, Yvonne Klein had refurbished the breakfast room and the lobby. But still a lot of things could be improved. That was the message the three students received before the start of their internship.

»In my first week, Ms. Klein told me to contribute my ideas and implement changes,« says Maralen Schiessl. »At first, that was a bit strange to me, because never before had I experienced something like that. After all, being in your early 20s, it is not often you are asked about your opinion when it comes to important decisions.« Initially, the students received an extensive introduction to the basics of the house, then were allowed to try themselves in all areas. The internal accounting system is – even for computer-savvy staff – a challenge, and clearing a table in two minutes is something to be learned, too. »Most questions can be solved with common sense,« says Yvonne Klein. If one of the new employees really gets stuck, Ms. Klein implements the same method she experienced with her mentor in Emden: »If one of the three students approaches me with a problem, I just ask them: ›How would you do this?‹ That's what helped me grow the most.«

»In the beginning, the guests of the hotel had to get accustomed to three Bavarians,« says Yvonne Klein.

»For the World Cup, we emptied the old restaurant, put in a TV, and served in Lederhosen,« Schwertfirm laughs.

»Meanwhile, many of our regular customers like the idea of having new students from Munich here,« says Klein. »Some even call beforehand and ask which of them will be in the house at which time.«

Schiessl, Fröhlich, and Schwertfirm developed new ideas for the re-alignment of the Seehotel Borkum, while still in Munich. »Before that, I had three internships in three different houses,« says Schwertfirm. »But these were mostly the usual activities. However, here in Borkum, we dug a little deeper.«

The Bavarians spent 20 percent of their time on strategic issues of the hotel. »It was important to us that the students would get a feel for high autonomy,« says Janssen. »Initially, they had the requirement to finance all investments from the income of the house. But their ideas were so good that, ultimately, we got a bank on board.« The students suggested the former dining room could be remodelled to a ›living room‹, which in the summer would serve as a lounge and in the winter could be transformed into a multi-function room. Part of the new concept of these three students was that the Seehotel should have a summer, as well as a winter season. Bodo Janssen, Yvonne Klein, and Dennis Schweikard approved the expansion. After the students had planned the strategy and the alteration, they prepared the financing documents for the bank. Janssen gave the papers the necessary fine-tuning, so the bank would easily give the Borkum hotel a loan of 150,000 euro as a grant for implementing the strategy.

»Even though we are no longer on site to witness the reconstruction, we are still in contact with our successors,« says Schwertfirm. »Ideally, we would have preferred to participate in the remodelling,« he adds wistfully. However, the next three students are preparing their trip to Borkum. Yvonne Klein also offers the conditions by which they can grow beyond themselves. »Here, they can have experiences which they would not get in the private sector too often,« Janssen says. He adds: »For us, as a company, it has ultimately paid off – we achieved double-digit sales and profit increases when we gave people the framework through which they could grow beyond themselves.«

Neuroplasticity in the adult brain

The head of HR of a Scandinavian energy company opened the worldwide change workshop, which I facilitated with content, with the words: »We are part of an industry that only knows ›grow‹ from the very beginning. For the first time in our history, we are in a crisis that is so existential that no one in our company can predict how we will earn our money in five years' time. And if we look at our competitors, it seems it is just the same with them.«

Not many industrial sectors are facing such a pronounced uncertain future as the energy industry. But in other areas of the economy as well, I encounter corporate leaders and managers, who realise they can't provide all the answers anymore. They are increasingly reliant on the creativity and solution-finding expertise of their teams. Eckes-Granini Germany and Heribert Gathof (from chapter 3) led the way. In this company, the strategy is not developed by management, but by the workforce. This trend is global; in 2010, a majority of 1,500 CEOs admitted in a worldwide IBM study: »The economic conditions are more complex than ever before, and we do not know how we will cope with this complexity. But we need the creativity of our employees to master this challenge.«

If managers want access to the creative potential of their employees, it helps to understand why experiences and neuroplasticity play such an important role.

1. Experiences and neuroplasticity increase stress resistance: A stronger cross-linked brain has more ways to respond to stress. The experience of the dm-drugstores' theatre workshops left neural links in the trainees' brains, which were accessible to them in their everyday lives. If the trainee must overcome the challenge to approach a customer, the neural pathways formed while being on stage and talking to several hundred people will help him. In another scenario, the trainee might experience problems with a customer, then the young person can use the neural networks he developed while working through a crisis with his fellow students in the workshop. When former British soldiers have to meet a tough deadline from their boss, they resort to the stress regulatory networks they developed during their combat operations.

Challenging experiences shape the neuroplasticity of our brains. The connections between individual nerve cells can be increased by so-called synaptic plasticity. Cortical plasticity forms new networks. In difficult situations, we can, therefore, rely on stable neural structures. This helps employees on two levels. First, through previously mastered challenges, they have already developed several synaptic connections and useful neural networks, which will support them when dealing with problems. Second, through many experiences, he developed a strong belief in his own abilities. Even if he finds no immediate solution to a problem, his belief in himself will give him the opportunity to view the problem as solvable. That helps the brain stay more relaxed in a stressful situation, which allows you to access your higher mental faculties.

2. Experiences and neuroplasticity increase creativity: Creative solutions and ideas are created when what you already know is connected in a new and unfamiliar way. In such moments, people connect neural networks not previously connected. However, for those networks to establish themselves in the first place, people need experience.

Would you trust yourself to build an anti-mosquito device in one of the world's malarial regions out of a DVD player, a laser printer and a webcam? Well, if you have experience with technology and know the basic building blocks of those three devices, you might come up with the same idea as the former computer hacker, Pablos Holman, and his friends a few years ago. The group used the photo module of the camera to detect mosquitoes. They could distinguish the harmless male from the malaria-transmitting female mosquitoes by their wing-beat frequency. The blue laser from the DVD player is aligned by the high-precision mirrors of the laser printer to the wings of the female mosquitoes. In one-tenth of a second, the high-energy blue laser vaporises the wings of a mosquito. It can no longer infect people with malaria. If Pablos Holman worked in a company, where he spent five years doing the same thing day in and day out, he would not have had sufficient experience nor would he have built the corresponding neural networks. However, Holman has had a varied career, which enabled him to put together the right thoughts so that he would now be able to install a fully automatic digital mosquito hunter in front of each hospital in a malaria-risk area.

To keep neuroplasticity in motion and create the basis for creativity, companies focus specifically on new experiences. The American company 3M ensures many employees work in different departments every five to seven years. The juice producer Eckes-Granini Germany allows its so-called Enterprise Groups (see chapter 3) from the logistics and IT department to solve problems for their colleagues in the sales department. The drugstore chain dm deploys

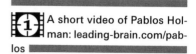 A short video of Pablos Holman: leading-brain.com/pablos

its trainees regularly to new stores, so they get to know how many things work. »I'm always surprised at how different my colleagues approach things in the other branches,« a trainee in his second year told me after having worked in three branches so far. »It shows me how differently we are allowed to work here.«

3. Experience and neuroplasticity enhance executive functions: For a moment, put your hand on your forehead. Behind the skin and bones lies a very special part of your brain: the prefrontal cortex (PFC). If a place in our brain is the equivalent of the word »potential« from the Circle of Potential, it's the PFC. It includes all the higher mental faculties you have already developed in your life or have yet to unfold: predictive action planning, empathy, the ability to distinguish between important and unimportant, impulse control, and the ability to think creatively.

As early as 1848 scientists suspected this part of the brain handled the higher mental faculties. The tragic protagonist of an event, back then, was railway worker Phineas Gage, the ancestor of well-known modern-day neuroscientist Fred Gage. In an unfortunate accident, Gage shot an iron rod through his left eye. The rod pierced his PFC and came out the other side of his head, then flew for another two meters. Miraculously, Phineas Gage survived. However, immediately after his heavy flesh wounds had healed, Gage showed personality changes. The previously very accessible man became irritable, a man who found it difficult to control his impulses and emotions. Scientists concluded from their observation, »This part of the brain must be the place of morality.« They are not completely wrong. With modern imaging methods, such as functional magnetic resonance imaging, we can show accurately that our PFC is very active when we use our higher mental faculties – our executive functions.

As I write these lines, I hear my little son, who came into this world

10 days ago, chortle in the next room. I feel the impulse to pick him up. However, because I have done that often already today, I control this impulse and continue to write. My PFC enables this impulse control. If I tuck him into bed at night, and perhaps, if he cries a little bit, I will think of something new to calm him. In this instance, too, I will fall back on my PFC and use its creative networks. Before I sit at my desk tomorrow morning, I will make my wife a nursing-tea, while she remains in bed with our baby. I do so, because the networks in my PFC enable me to empathise with my son, who has suffered from abdominal pain over the last few days. And the anticipator/predictive action planning of my PFC makes it possible that today, I can think of what I will do tomorrow to ease my son's discomfort.

In March, my publisher expects the finished manuscript for this book, and I have decided not to accept any further jobs until then. However, I know my customers well. Quite a few will call me because something »very important« is about to happen. Every time, I will have to decide whether to take this job or ask one of my partners from our advisory group, so I can spend this time with my son and this manuscript. The evaluation of »important« and »less important« also takes place in my PFC.

Just for a moment, think of your employees. Perhaps, among them, there are some who you wish could distinguish between important and unimportant. Maybe you can also think of someone who would benefit from more empathy and attentiveness. Would you, perhaps, like more focus on solutions, instead of a »blame culture«? The foundation to access those skills or to develop more of them is neurobiologically present in every human being. The networks can form and structure themselves at any time. Think of hotel director Dennis Schweikard, the young hotel manager Yvonne Klein, the three students of the Munich Academy, or the trainees from the drugstore chain dm. Companies must create the conditions under which people are encouraged to gain new experiences, so their brains can build new networks.

Why doesn't every experience subsequently create neuroplastic changes?

Fred Gage, the descendant of accident victim Phineas Gage, who shot an iron bar through his PFC, was one of the leading researchers of a subcategory of neuroplasticity: adult neurogenesis, the ability of the adult brain to produce new neurons. He was part of a small group of selected scientists allowed to visit the Dalai Lama in his Indian exile in Dharamsala. The main theme of this annual meeting in 2004 between His Holiness and science was neuroplasticity. Gage had already published a study in 1997 in which he reported the impact of so-called »enriched environments« in the brains of rodents.

He divided mice into two groups. Group one lived in a normal laboratory animal cage, without any equipment. Group two enjoyed an »Enriched Environment«: wheels, tunnels, toys, plenty of room for other mice, and many opportunities for social interaction. After 40 days in this environment, Gage and his colleagues detected that the mice from the cages with more experience opportunities had a 15 percent higher neurogenesis in the hippocampus. This made Gage one of the leading scientists in the field of the effect of experience on the brain.

However, in 2004, he reported another study, in which the Dalai Lama and the monks became very much interested. Gage discovered that, besides the »Enriched Environments,« even the simplest physical exercise can have a positive influence on the formation of new nerve cells. Scientists kept genetically identical mice in cages, with and without running wheels. An active mouse covered several kilometres easily in a day – or even at night – in its wheel. After a short time, the active mice showed increased formation of new nerve cells, compared to the mice without a wheel. A small additional experiment interested the Buddhist audiences: The researchers, with the help of technical means, prevented some of the active mice from getting out of the wheel again; they had to run constantly. As Gage compared the brains of the voluntary and involuntary runners, he noted mice that had to run had no increase in brain mass. Neurogenesis did not happen when the exercise was involuntary. Among the animals that exercised voluntarily, not only had they produced measurably more brain cells, they were also more intelligent. In a subsequent test, the mice that could run freely achieved better results than did the other group of mice, which were forced to run.

The realisation of this experiment: The brain changes with experience, but only if this is voluntary. Involuntary experiences release stress, which often prevents a restructuring of the brain!

We now know the impact of stress on our brains is worse than what was thought in 2004: If people perform involuntary actions over too long a period of time and are exposed to severe stress, a frightening form of neuroplasticity occurs: Deconstruction. Some neural networks then dissolve. Some areas of the hippocampus – the »librarian« of our brains – disintegrate. The decline of these networks comes with unpleasant consequences: The »librarian« has only a limited ability to store and retrieve information. This becomes obvious to the person as they lose their ability to learn, which affects their memory. This is known as stress-related forgetfulness.

People need controllable stress experiences

There is hardly any word in the professional and private environment used as often to describe personal unease as the term »stress.« The German federal government even published a Stress Report in which it informed citizens about where we and our stress (issues) are. In addition, insurance companies present annual reports about the billions of euro lost each year due to stress-related absences.

All that is true, yet at the same time, we need stress. Similar to medicine, it is the dose that determines whether stress does us good or harm. We are always exposed to small and large stressors, also called stress-causing stimuli: a car which will not start in the morning or a wife who wants to apply a »bit of make-up« quickly, even though you wanted to leave ten minutes ago. There's the husband, who did not put the food back in the fridge, the traffic jam on the way to work, the medical findings by the family doctor. How about the promotion, the long-hoped-for project responsibility, or the important business trip to Asia?

Each of these stressors causes your brain to activate its central noradrenergic system, a network of neuronal structures responsible for the production, storage, and release of noradrenaline. If the stressor is also enjoyable, the brain releases dopamine in addition to noradrenaline. If you transferred a very important project to an employee, something he had wanted to take on for a long time, his noradrenergic and dopaminergic system would become active: He would be happy, but he would also feel great responsibility. However, for another employee, the internal audit department knocks on his door, wanting the documents from the penultimate year within a week. The noradrenergic system is activated – you can safely assume the dopaminergic system is not activated. You have two people with two stressors. One of the stressors is rather pleasant: the desired project responsibility. The other is rather unpleasant: the auditors put pressure on the employee.

Let's look at ways to create good neuroplastic solutions for the brain. First, not all solutions acceptable to the brain are optimal for the social environment. But more on that later ...

Your employee, who has to deal with the audit request, could meet with the internal auditor for lunch, strengthen the relationship with him, and discuss, in this more informal atmosphere, which of the requested documents are actually relevant and whether the deadline could be slightly moved back. Should he succeed with this strategy, the nonspecific noradrenergic arousal in his brain will decrease, while the neural networks he had used to solve the problem will strengthen. When we are exposed to a stressor and find a solution for it, we experience a controlled stress response. If we have mastered the problem, our brains release chemical messengers that stabilise the neural networks used to solve the problem. This is an ideal course of a neuroplastic process.

Socially incompatible, but in terms of brain function just as effective, is the following alternative: Your employee calls his colleagues from the audit department and insults them on the phone, yelling at them that they are stealing his time: »I am here to make money and not to do the groundwork for you bean counters.« Then the situation escalates: The head of the audit calls you to complain about your staff member. »My office – a word,« you tell the employee, who whines that due to the heavy workload he simply does not have time for this extra administrative work. You decide to sack him and delegate the work for the audit department to another employee. In the brain of your employee, the unspecific noradrenergic arousal decreases and stabilises the networks that have contributed to solving the problem. In a future similar situation, the same network will be activated: First scream, then whine. In terms of brain functions, that works wonderfully to reduce stress.

If you, as his boss, go along with it every time such a situation occurs, your employee does not need to look for another solution: For him, on a neural level, to use the existing networks saves more energy than forming new networks.

When we are exposed to a stressor and find a solution to it, we experience a controlled stress response. If we have mastered the problem, our brains release chemical messengers that stabilise the neural networks used to solve the problem. This is an ideal course for a neuroplastic process.

For completeness, however, we should also look at the second option: the uncontrollable stress response. Whether a stress reaction is controllable or uncontrollable depends on how the person experiences and deals with the stressor. (See chapter 3: Three ways to increase stress resistance.)

Let's stay with the staff member to whom you have passed on the long-awaited project. His initial response activates the noradrenergic and dopaminergic systems – the latter because he is very happy and this project is highly meaningful to him. It's the dopaminergic system that gives him the stamina and motivation to work for weeks to come, day and night, on this project. The first interim report to the board is due in a month's time. Working day and night on this project takes its toll: The motivation created by the dopamine is strong, but the higher mental performance of his PFC is without rest and, therefore, not nearly as functioning as it could be. Your employee gets lots of details about the project which, at the moment, are less important. His overtired PFC can no longer reliably differentiate between important and unimportant due to fatigue. He realises he is behind schedule: The once-useful noradrenergic arousal is now in overdrive. This leads some of the younger prefrontal networks to fail. They take over some of the older, more stable networks of the PFC, which the individual developed at age 10, 7 or 5. No longer does he represent his best and most mature adult self. Your staff member realises this project is getting out of hand. However, instead of sleeping and getting some much-needed rest, he shifts up a gear and works even harder. Without new energy reserves, the PFC can no longer control the growing fear of the approaching deadline and possible failure. It does not cross the mind of your employee to ask for help as a second approach to stress resistance. The initially controllable stress situation has become an uncontrollable stress response. The hypothalamus has activated, via the pituitary gland, the adrenal glands, and these have started the production of a stress cocktail of adrenaline and cortisol. The body of your employee responds with a faster heartbeat and a change in the digestive system. Biologically, all alarms bells are ringing. His hippocampus, the »librarian« of the brain, is attacked by the stress cocktail from the adrenal glands. If that happens for a prolonged period, the hippocampus withdraws its connections to the other parts of the brain. That the »librarian« of the head can no longer store or retrieve information is a disturbing notion. Your employee is now noticeably overwhelmed.

Experiences are needed in the right dose. If an experience is not demanding enough, your noradrenergic system remains inactive: The brain is far away from any neuroplastic experience. If the experience is too demanding, and your employee cannot get outside help or comfort himself by saying and believing »that it all will work out,« his brain goes into overdrive, which will temporarily lead to a limited function of his PFC. He slips into a neural alarm mode, and if this period lasts too long, into a symptom called burnout.

Essence for Executives

Experience – People grow when they are challenged

- Experience shapes neuronal networks and the internal pictures of people. Positive internal pictures influence the unfolding of their »hidden« potential. People can grow beyond themselves.
- »We achieved double-digit revenue and profit growth after we created a framework that allowed all our employees to grow beyond themselves,« says Upstalsboom owner Bodo Janssen.
- Experiences have to be voluntary. Once people behave under pressure, only minor restructuring of the neural networks, little learning, and hardly any personal growth take place. At worst, neural networks are destroyed by the experienced stress.
- In the drugstore chain dm, all learners participate in eight-day theatre workshops. They have experiences that go far beyond their usual workday, which later gives them more confidence when dealing with

customers. »Some of us have already grown far beyond themselves,« says trainee Felix Woller.

- If people regularly master challenges, this will increase their belief in themselves and increase their resilience.
- It needs the right level of experience: If challenges are too undemanding, no neuroplasticity takes place. If a person feels overwhelmed for a long period, this will trigger a so-called uncontrollable stress response, while access to their higher intellectual achievements decreases.

Chapter 6

Meaningfulness – People get access to their resources

»I sell not only our bread but the entire spirit of our company.«

Sabine Jansen, Sales Director, Märkisches Landbrot

On September 27, 1973, at 22:45, the phone rang at Siegfried Steiger's. The call came from Bonn. On the other end of the line was Prof. Dr. Horst Ehmke, the German Federal Minister of Post and Telecommunications. »I'm still sitting at the Chancellor's. We had a meeting with the federal states' prime ministers. You will be happy to hear we have decided on the emergency call number – your stubbornness has prevailed!«

At last, the long-awaited and hard-fought-for decision was made. Siegfried Steiger and his wife, Ute, had kept many politicians at the federal and state level on their toes throughout the years. Finally, the architect couple had obtained a political decision, which would increase the chances of survival and physical safety for all citizens: a single emergency number for the whole of Germany. What appears normal today was not possible some years ago, because it was said to be »impossible to finance« on a political level: In 1973, just 150 of more than 3,700 local telephone networks had one single emergency number. Usually, the larger cities were better supplied, though. If you lived outside those 150 networks and wanted to make an emergency call, you first had to search the phone book for the number of the nearest hospital or police station. People lost valuable time, which could make the difference between life and death. On her typewriter, Ute Steiger had written over 6,000 letters to the political authorities. For the region of north Wurttemberg, the couple was able, with the help of local politicians, to fund and implement the emergency numbers 110 and 112. With this action, they refuted the argument that a lack of financing was a legitimate impediment to their goal. However, for the rest of Germany, politicians still didn't want to participate. After state and federal politicians repeatedly pushed responsibility onto each other and continued refusing to make this life-saving decision, Siegfried Steiger sued the the State of Baden-Wurttemberg as a representative of the whole country of Germany.

Dr. Siegfried Kasper, the judge in charge of the Administrative Court of Stuttgart, was forced to dismiss the application on technical legal grounds, even though he personally would have liked to decide otherwise. Decades later, he recalls: »As a young judge, I thought the issue was important. That's why I conducted a public hearing to which I invited the press.« Kasper, before his official judicial decision in which he dismissed the action, made a long plea for the need for the emergency number; the attending journalists had a field day! The media attention, subsequently, led to the implementation of the 110 number, says Kasper. Finally, the politicians could no longer resist the public pressure; the political decision took place six months after the trial. »Although he annoyed us, that was exactly what led him to success,« retired minister, Horst Ehmke recalls. The long, hard road was worth it.

What persuaded the Steigers to take on politicians of all stripes to enforce their concerns? Friedrich Nietzsche explains it with these words: »He who has a Why to live can bear almost any How.« The »why« the Steigers found tragically when their son, Björn, was hit by a car on his way home only one week before his ninth birthday. If the rescue system had been better in 1969, Björn Steiger would have survived. The actual injury was not life-threatening. However, because the ambulance arrived one hour later, Björn died of shock. »All he needed to survive was some oxygen,« says his father, Siegfried Steiger.

Imagine you had an accident in the year 1970. If you were on a country road, you would have had to wait until another motorist passed by. He then would have driven to the next town to call an ambulance. He would need enough change in his pocket for the phone booth, because after finding the right number in the phone book, he would have to call several hospitals. Back then, only a few clinics had a suitable transport vehicle. What would happen next was what was literally called the »rearview mirror rescue«: A single driver with, most likely, not more than basic first aid training would come to the accident site, put you on a stretcher, and take you off to the hospital. During the trip, he would watch you and your condition in the rear-view mirror.

»Back then, like most other people we asked, we did not know there was no ambulance service in Germany,« says Siegfried Steiger. »It was not until the day after Björns' accident that we learned about it, and we immediately agreed: We have to do something.« The couple founded the Björn Steiger Foundation and revolutionised the German ambulance system. »Just imagine, back then, they didn't even have radios in their ambulances,« he says. »One of our first concerns was to change that. Nationwide, we collected wastepaper and sold it to finance the radios. Back then, the price of such a device was about 7,500 Deutsche Mark.« The Björn Steiger foundation not only made the 112 number come true, but equipped many ambulances with radios. In addition, it financed the first mobile intensive care unit of the republic. Steiger recalls: »The idea was to donate this unit through the BILD-Zeitung [Germanys biggest newspaper]. The only condition we had: The mobile intensive care unit had to be staffed 24/7. Not a single community in the entire country answered. Finally, a handful of Stuttgart hospitals came together. Each committed to providing a doctor for the car on different days of the month.«

The Björn Steiger Foundation eventually bought the first rescue helicopter in the country and contributed with financial support and numerous political campaigns to ensure Germany today is one of best resourced countries in the world regarding medical emergencies. To ensure other people would not suffer the same fate they did became the driver for the couple. This force is so extraordinary those two people have fought for the safety of others for the last 40 years.

When people experience meaningfulness, they endure challenging circumstances more easily. This also applies to everyday situations. Increased, experienced meaningfulness gives access to one's own resources and is an incentive for an upsurge in performance, as the behavioural economist Dan Ariely and psychology professor Adam Grant will prove in the following. Especially in the working environment, the search for meaning is becoming more important. A progressive shift in consciousness, a new value system among Generation Y, and declining existential threats may be the driving force behind it.

150 years ago, (work-) life was much harder for many people. Yet, they also experienced a symbiosis of work and social environment as it barely exists in the Western world, today. In this community setting, it was an everyday experience for the miller and the baker that their products nourished the people of their village. The carpenter could see the result of his work during a walk through the town, and the tailor rejoiced in creating his clothes, which his fellow citizens wore. With the beginning of industrialisation, this working concept transformed. If someone worked in a factory, the results of their labours were no longer a direct benefit to his community. An initially important aspect of work, namely to contribute something to one's own community, gradually disappeared.

Even though »contributing« and »giving something to other people« is a quality that deeply satisfies us, Lara Aknin of the University of British Columbia in Canada demonstrated, in a study published in 2012, that this behaviour led to increased personal satisfaction, even for two-year infants. Well-trained assistants observed the facial expressions of children during an experiment and could deduce how happy the kids were. When the children received sweets, they rejoiced. However, if they could share their candy with a toy monkey, their observable happiness was greater. Similar experiments with adults led to comparable results. Lara Aknin and her colleague, Elisabeth Dunn, interviewed people regarding their personal happiness. The interviewees could indicate their answers on a scale system, so changes could be measured more easily. Subsequently, the two researchers gave each of the surveyed people an envelope with a small sum of money. Half of the participants were instructed to spend the money on themselves, while the other half was asked to spend it on something good for other people. At night, the scientists interviewed all participants by phone. Those who spent the money on other people reported considerably higher growth on the happiness scale than those who had spent the money on themselves.

Märkisches Landbrot | Baking within the brotherhood

Berlin-Neukölln's mayor, Heinz Buschkowsky, awarded the manager of the Märkisches Landbrot, Joachim Weckmann, the Federal Cross of Merit, and even partly supported the company with public money. I asked Heinz Buschkowsky to tell me in a few words why the Märkisches Landbrot was so close to his heart. The length of his answer surprised me, because Buschkowsky had plenty of other things to do, since he had announced his retirement from politics only a few days earlier:

When you talk about the company Märkisches Landbrot, you cannot do so in isolation from its »spiritus rector,« the very likeable and charismatic Joachim Weckmann. He embodies the organic philosophy even better than any commercial with blooming fields. You blindly believe the quality of his products increases when the regional grain is ground fresh on stone mills and the water comes from private wells. ›Bread is a process, not a finished product.‹ That's how he always begins his explanation for groups of visitors when he talks about the difference of the Märkisches Landbrot as opposed to other bakeries. Next, you get to feel his enthusiasm. When he explains that, for preparing the Märkisches Landbrot, the water for the dough is first energised through the teachings of Feng Shui, which leads to a measurable difference compared to the now very common inflation technique of so-called fresh bakeries, only then are you able to distinguish quality from frozen dough from Indonesia. For the low-cost ›bakeries‹ he has some fine-cut words: ›If people knew what they were doing by putting those products into their bodies, that would spell the end of this industry from one day to the next.‹ Sure, his bread costs a few cents more. But it tastes better, and people live a little healthier, he smiles to himself. By the way, my tip is the carrot and walnut bread. You hardly need to put anything on top of your slice.

For a man like Joachim Weckman, it goes without saying that he received the Federal Cross of Merit, and there is no social event in his district that he would deny requested support. He is a great guy.

In 2007, Heinz Buschkowsky invested public money, so the organic bakery could make its exemplary work better known. With a subsidy of 8,000 euro, the company built a small visitor centre to offer tours, informing the public about the operation. »We now count nearly 8,000 visitors per year,« said Jürgen Baumann, who is leading those people through the 50-man operation. »Among the guests are kindergarteners, who learn about healthy eating, students whose teachers shop in the health food store and who want to convey knowledge of healthy nutrition up close, right down to the company representatives, who want to know more about our company culture. We feel a social change, especially because the group of young adult visitors steadily grows. The fact that more company representatives come to our tours reflects a growing awareness of better economies.« Works Council chairman Patrick Hannemann says: »If, at the end of such a tour, you meet the group once again, that indeed is a nice feeling. You never see an unhappy face. Particularly exciting was the visit by Japanese state television.« Sometimes, Operations Manager Katja Pampel leads the tours. She is the specialist in the »carbon footprint« calculator that can be found on the company's website. There, every customer can work out for himself how much CO_2 each bread consumes. The results vary from year to year because of, for example, fluctuating harvest capacities or wet years in which the grain must be dried after harvesting. »I am proud that many people and visitors perceive us as a sustainable business,« she told me.

Enterprise: Märkisches Landbrot GmbH
Industry: Organic bakery
Headquarters: Berlin, Germany
Established: 1930
Employees: 49
Website: www.landbrot.de
Noteworthy: The company is committed to the highest social and environmental standards. If the company's profit exceeds a fixed quota, the money will be used to increase staff wages, to keep product prices low, or to pay suppliers even better.

CEO Joachim Weckmann adds: »We sense that as a form of respect, so many people want to see what we are doing here. It is an appreciation for what we have stood for through the decades.« Many of the staff become accustomed to the curious glances thrown over their shoulders while working. »If it's not rush hour, colleagues are always happy to answer questions,« says Jürgen Baumann.

The company motto, »There is always a beginning for something better,« characterises not only the multi-award-winning bread of the organic bakery, but the work on a human level – both internally and externally – and has done so for three decades. A few years ago, a miller, a supplier of Märkisches Landbrot, was on the verge of bankruptcy. He had his offices in a structurally weak region. Weckmann gave him the money he needed to pay his debts, and employed him at the bakery. »Of course, we cannot constantly lend money. Until recently, we too had a larger sum to pay off at our bank,« says Weckmann. Nevertheless, he loaned money again to a competitor – an organic bakery in Berlin denied by the banks for transitional financing. »Brotherhood, for me, is an important part of our approach, to which we are committed as a ›Demeter‹ company [a German anthroposophical organic alliance],« Weckmann says, upholding his decisions fervently. »After all, throughout my life, I have been through many difficult situations, where other people believed in me and helped me.«

Weckmann came to West Berlin in 1976. With completed business studies under his belt, he was strongly influenced by the 1968 movement. »Like many other people around me, back then, I cooked food for others and sold it,« he says, remembering his first time in the city, which was still surrounded by the GDR. Together, with some like-minded people, he founded a baker collective. He always felt a great closeness to the Socialists, and so he became co-founder of the first Berlin organic bakery. He moved to another collective, which he soon left as well: »In 1981, I was out, because they refused to supply the KaDeWe department store. ›Good bread serves everyone – no matter where people buy it‹ was my attitude towards this matter. But the other members of the collective saw it differently.« I had a fair idea of what he meant, but still asked him: »What would have been so bad about delivering bread to the KaDeWe?« Even though over 30 years have passed since then, quick as a shot, he replied: »High finance. That was always the class enemy.« Then he has to laugh at himself. He has kept his clear values to this day. During one of our conversations in early January 2015, the bearded 62-year-old asked me: »On Saturday, you'll also come to the protest against genetic engineering and TTIP, right?«

After he had separated from his old collectives in 1981, because they would not provide bread for the »class enemy,« he spread his wings.

With the help of a loan, he bought the Berlin-Neukölln-based bakery »Märkisches Landbrot«, which had been established in 1930. »I was highly politically minded,« Weckmann recalls. »With my own business, I could consistently live up to my vision and manufacture products in a way that fit the values of ›Solidarity and Sustainability.‹«

Weckmann not only designed the bakery, according to his values, but gathered numerous like-minded entrepreneurs around him. In this way, the Märkisches Landbrot became the cornerstone for the entire industry. Together, they developed a special range of organic foods, with a growing number of customers willing to pay for health and sustainability. In addition, the management team of the Märkisches Landbrot established work environments for themselves and for their partner companies, considered more liveable than »big business.« »Initially, I was very critical,« Operations Manager Katja Pampel told me. »I thought everything I had read about the Märkisches Landbrot was pure marketing. Nonetheless, I was curious to work there. Ultimately, I learned there was a lot of ›substance‹ behind all those initiatives. In particular, the environmental management goes far beyond what one would expect from a bakery.«

»As a work council, we do not really have much to do,« Patrick Hannemann told me. »But you have to be honest. To the outside, it looks as if our company had a very structured approach to everything. Internally, however, we are often quite chaotic.« Hannemann is one of three employees who celebrated their 25th anniversary in 2015. »I always said I would leave only if the work here in the bakery was not enjoyable for more for three successive months. So far, that has not happened.«

The Corporate Social Responsibility (CSR), which some companies establish these days, has been, at Märkisches Landbrot, part of the company's DNA since 1981. In 1992, the bakery created its first company ecological balance sheet, while a year later, it reduced its CO_2 emissions by 60 percent. In 1994, the company received the first Eco Audit Certificate in the food industry and committed itself to pursuing a continuous improvement process under the principle of sustainability. Just three years later, the bakery received the Berlin Environmental Award. »Joachim tried a lot,« says employee Jürgen Baumann. »The purpose of my work strengthened measurably. We are a bread producer, and bread is one of the most important staple foods in the number-one ›bread country.‹ This makes you feel all right.«

In 2008, when more medium-sized and listed companies systematically made CSR part of their corporate strategy, Märkisches Landbrot published their CSR concept as the first German bakery to do so. »I like the social commitment here a lot,« says Katja Pampel. »Besides, I can fully stand behind what the company and I, as an employee, are doing. It is important to find meaning in what I do.«

»Which of your numerous organic-initiatives is closest to your heart?« I asked Weckmann during a train ride.

»The Märkische Economic Network, with its ›fair & regional‹ initiative, is important to me,« he replies. »We must begin to see each other, once again, as brothers and sisters and treat each other accordingly.«

Fair & regional is an initiative that became a model for similar organisations throughout the country. Among the 48 mutually certified members of the Berlin-Brandenburg region are producers (farmers), processors (bakeries), and distributors. They meet regularly at a round table to discuss supplies and prices and any problems to arrive at a single solution. In 2009, the members of the »grain round table« freed their agreed prices from the fluctuating world market prices. The ongoing stock market speculation on resources had nothing to do with the reality in the area around Berlin. By replacing speculative prices, all participants received economic security and could plan for the long term. »If, things get tight for any of the members, sometimes we pay even earlier. There is cash flow, regardless of the flow of goods,« says Weckmann. »For us, in the bakery, that means a bit more effort. We would have fewer problems if we just bought the grain where the quality is best. That would mean at different places each year. To always buy within the region means we repeatedly struggled with the fluctuation of quality.«

A consumer who chooses products with the »fair & regional« seal can inform himself about all agreements between the members. The minutes of all meetings of the association are published on the company's website. For example, in the minutes from June 11, 2014, you can read the management team of Märkisches Landbrot was thinking about new sales channels, that some farmers had problems with plant diseases, and that an organic bakery was restructuring and planned to buy silos. The 25 participants of the meeting discussed, according to the minutes, the quality problems with rye, the current short supply of spelt, and the positive customer response to »champagne rye.« You also learn that the processing plants took from farmers the amounts agreed in 2013, even though their own demand was lower. The bought-but-not-needed grain was sold on by the bakeries. Finally, the companies published an agreement to increase the purchase prices by five percent. »I feel we maintain a friendly relationship with each other,« says Katja Pampel. »There are always situations where farmers have the opportunity to sell their grain elsewhere for a better price. We treat each other as equals.« Sabine Jansen, sales director in the field, added: »Most of our customers buy our bread because of its quality. I believe the impact of all our initiatives makes up 20 percent of the purchasing decisions. The greater influence is on us, the employees. I sell not only our bread, but the entire spirit of our company.«

Since 2002, the Märkisches Landbrot has fulfilled another part of its social responsibility with the »Organic-Bread Box.« The bakery is co-initiator of an idea that reaches more than 170,000 pupils nationwide. »Initially, the bread from the Bread Box came only from us,« says master baker Hannemann. »By now, all other Berlin organic bakeries participate as well.« It started in Berlin: To give pupils and parents a better understanding of healthy eating, all Berlin first graders received, at the beginning of the year, a lunchbox filled with organic food. In England, British celebrity chef Jamie Oliver started a similar initiative a few years later. He consistently improved the diets of students in selected schools. Due to its popularity and media presence, some scientists took on his project and could show that a healthy diet not only cuts down on the sick days of students, but has a positive effect on grades.

»All this dedication, is that economically viable for your business?« I want to know from Joachim Weckmann.

»We are thinking differently,« he replies. »We do not want to make huge profits, but cap our operating cash flow at 15 percent. We committed to 15 percent. Everyone can read that on our website. There are bakeries that achieve 30 percent. If we arrive at 15 percent, we do something. We invest in something, so the bread stays at a low cost, or we pay our suppliers better, or raise the wages of our employees. They are, anyhow, in the upper third of the industry,« Weckmann told me during one of our last conversations. Then he suddenly opened up to another, very different matter: »It becomes increasingly difficult for our employees to find apartments close to the company.« The Berlin-Neukölln neighbourhood is becoming more attractive and gentrification – the exodus of the less wealthy and the influx of the wealthier population – does not stop here.

»I have always been Neuköllner through and through,« Hannemann told me. »But what has happened in the neighbourhood for several years is not good for many people. You pay rent now of up to 13 euro per square metre. Who can really afford that?« Even the management did not like that their employees – particularly the night shift – had to commute great distances because of these high rental rates. Therefore, Joachim Weckmann, with two colleagues, purchased a classic Berlin building with high ceilings in the direct vicinity of the Neukölln shipping canal, just a few minutes from the bakery. Whenever an apartment in the house becomes vacant, the employees of Märkisches Landbrot receive an offer at a rental price of about 6 euro per square metre. »Just recently, I moved into such an apartment,« says Sabine Jansen. »I would not find anything for a similar rent around here. However, if we want to maintain the same high standards as the company, we have to make a few ecological adjustments in the house,« she adds with a laugh. »That rocks!« Hannemann commented in the purest Berlin dialect. »If an employer does something like that, it's simply world-class!«

»Someone who is not doing anything for others does not do anything for themselves« (Johann Wolfgang von Goethe)

That entrepreneurs want to do good is nothing new. In 1953, a lawsuit took place before the New Jersey Supreme Court, giving a company the legal basis to apply itself in a non-profit manner. A shareholder of the Standard Oil Company sued the enterprise, because it »wasted« money through a multimillion-dollar donation to Princeton University. Standard Oil supported the university financially to maintain the quality of education at a level the company expected of future graduates and potential employees. The risk that Princeton students could also work for other companies was one that Standard Oil was willing to take. Therefore, the shareholder had no immediate benefit by the donation. The Supreme Court ruled, at that time, in favour of Standard Oil and allowed the high donation to Princeton University for benevolent purposes. The court decision paved the way for countless other companies that could give similarly large sums, without a directly recognisable value.

In the 70s, the well-known economist and management advisor Peter Drucker argued companies should commit themselves to social activities for the benefit of society. Many classical theories of motivation and human development in the last century (conducted by scientists such as psychologist Abraham Maslow in the 1950s and 70s, MIT professor Douglas McGregor in the 60s, behavioural and social psychologist David McClelland in the 60s, and founder of the Third Viennese School of Psychotherapy Viktor Frankl in the 60s and 70s) suggest that people are looking for more than financial security and social recognition. Frankl made man's search for meaning the focus of his »meaning-centred psychology.« The Canadian babies in Lara Aknin's study underpin how deep our quest for meaningful actions is embedded in us: To share one's own food with a toy monkey increased the perceived happiness of young children measurably.

In 2008, two researchers looked closely at the by-now large field of scientific papers about Corporate Social Responsibility. Herman Aguinis, professor of Organisational Behaviour & Human Resources, and his colleague Ante Glavas from the University of Notre Dame analysed 588 articles and 102 book chapters devoted to this topic. The definition of CSR is clearly defined: It is the commitment of a company to reducing potential adverse effects on society and to increase the long-term positive impact on society. Apart from all the obvious and now demonstrable impacts, such as an improved image, increased sales, and more satisfied shareholders, the scientists could detect something further: In a business with a clear CSR strategy, there is also a measurable positive change in the attitudes of employees towards their company.

Stefan Raub from the École hôtelière de Lausanne issued a matching study, which went one step further. Raub showed that employees not only changed their attitudes, but also measurably changed their behaviour. In total, 211 employees from four hotels in several English cities participated in Raub's research. Among the most important issues of the Swiss researcher was the question of how much staff knew of the CSR activities of their company. Only when people know their employer does good can they react to it. After the surveys, evaluations, and interpretations, Raub came to the following conclusion:

The realisation: Employees who are aware of the CSR activities of their own company and its subsequent positive impact, first, show a greater willingness to help colleagues, second, give considerably more constructive proposals to improve work processes and, third, feel less fatigue than those colleagues who know nothing about the CSR activities of the company.

In countries outside the western hemisphere, scientists are also studying the effects of the social commitment of a company to its own employees. The management scientist Imran Ali from IQRA University Islamabad in Pakistan published a study in 2010, entitled »Corporate Social Responsibility Influences, employee's commitment organisational performance.« The study, which was published in the African Journal of Business Management, mentions: »Researchers are advising corporations to consider the amount spent on CSR as investment, rather than expenses.«

Five minutes for more meaningfulness – and better performance

Adam Grant, in his late 20s, was the youngest professor of psychology at the Wharton University of Pennsylvania. Business Week listed him as one of only a few »Favourite Professors«, and he was chosen by the British HR Magazine as the »Most Influential International Thinker.« The amateur magician, again and again, surprises with his research. In 2006, he conducted a study that impressively proved how meaningfulness can double the motivation of a person within a few minutes. Grant did not conduct his study in the lab, but in an ordinary company. He and his colleagues began with the hypothesis that the endurance of an employee can be increased, when he encounters respectful human contact, which has an immediate benefit on the work done.

Grant chose employees of a call centre for his study. This job holds a high potential for frustration, because partly, employees are treated in a very unfriendly manner by callers. The staff was to collect donations for a public university from former students. Because they called people mainly in the evenings, some felt their privacy was disturbed, and with no hesitation, let the call centre staff know about it.

The scientists divided the employees, without them knowing it, into three groups. They wanted to investigate the influence it would have on the staff if they met a student who had received a scholarship from the university, a scholarship partially funded by donations raised by the call centre.

Group one received direct contact with this student. Group two had only indirect contact, while group three had no contact.

One day, group one was called to a brief meeting with the team leader. The team leader informed his staff that »by serendipity« one of the students receiving a scholarship from the university was in the house. His scholarship was possible only through the donations they had collected. The student was asked to participate in the meeting, and staff had five minutes to converse with him. This created a situation in which the employees were able to learn about the positive influence their work had. Without them, the student would not have received the scholarship.

Here you can learn more about Adam Grant: leading-brain.com/grant

The team leader told group two that a student with the scholarship had written a letter, thanking staff for their work, which had made the scholarship possible. Those employees were given a letter and had five minutes to discuss the content of the letter.

Adam Grant had agreed with the company in advance that two indicators should be documented: 1. The time staff spent on the phone, two weeks before the experiment and four weeks after the experiment, should be measured; 2. The collected donations would be measured throughout the same period. From group three, the control group, no change was expected. The key indicators of group one made a giant leap. Those five minutes of meaningfulness they received during the meeting with the student who received the scholarship meant their time spent on the phone increased by 142 percent, and the money they collected increased by 171 percent.

»Wolfgang Schäuble (Germany's minister of finance) is the only one in Berlin who receives salt from us,« says Markus Dornseif. »In the whole city, on public as well as private properties, it is strictly prohibited to scatter salt in the winter. However, there is a special permit for the wheelchair of the Minister, for the few metres from the rear of his car to the Ministry of Finance. There we sprinkle salt. For the driver, the special permit is not valid; on the side of the driver's door, there's no salt.« Markus Dornseif is part of the management of the winter service of the same name, Dornseif & Kfr – by far, the largest player in the industry, with over 19,000 properties to take care of.

Company: Dornseif e.Kfr.
Industry: Winter services
Headquarters: Münster, Germany
Established: 2001
Employees: 40
Website: www.dornseif.de
Noteworthy: Dornseif made its own corporate culture into a product: Dream Work. All employees create Dream Work jointly and work with a high degree of emotional bonding at the winter service company.

The boss seems to cope with cold temperatures well. »Do you mind me opening the window?« he asks at the beginning of our meeting in his office. It is February 2015, and the outside temperature is just above zero degrees. After having made it through the first 30 minutes of our conversation, I ask Dornseif to close the window.

In 2013, when Gerald Hüther and I published the first results of our joint work on remarkable corporate cultures, an employee of Dornseif contacted me. »We are an exceptional company, too,« she wrote. »But if I share all the reasons, it would fill a book.« Eighteen months later, I finally had time to look more closely at this company on the outskirts of Münster. Meanwhile, Liz Mohn, the grey eminence of the Bertelsmann enterprise, and Federal Minister Andrea Nahles met with Markus Dornseif. So far, Dornseif is one of only seven German companies presented with the newly formed INQA Certification – Initiative New Quality at the workplace. Of these seven companies, Dornseif was the only one who has undergone and passed the complete certification.

»In this company, I have the same feeling as in my family,« Ömer Tekin told me. He works in the disposition and usually starts at 2 a.m., so that in the morning, the 11 million square meters Dornseif oversees Germany-wide is free of snow. He is Muslim and prays five times a day. Tekin works with his colleagues from the disposition in the operations centre, a large room with many small and large monitors, resembling a trading floor – a rather inappropriate place to pray. »With my previous employer, I always had to go in the stairwell to pray, although there were enough empty rooms,« he says. »However, here, I can go to the archive in the summer. In the winter, though, it is too cold. Now, the management assistant wrote me a sign: ›Islamic Prayer Room.‹ Morning Prayer is between 6:30 and 7:30 am. Sometimes, it can get really hectic in the disposition, and I forget about prayer. Then my team leader comes to me and reminds me: ›Ömer, it's time.‹« Tekin then finds an empty office and hangs his prayer sign on the door. His colleagues know they must stay out for the time being.

»Smile,« says the display on the desk phone. I am talking to Ralf Stückenschneider. He works in the accounting department and seems a bit shyer than his colleagues, who, through the closed door, I hear running down the hallway, laughing. »I feel that I am welcome here,« he tells me. »I worked in planning, but that was not a good match. After the trial period, the company could have dismissed me, but instead, they offered me the job in accounting. That's the best thing that could have happened to me.«

Stückenschneider has now been with the company for nearly three years and still marvels at how ›super easy‹ the guys are with each other. If he really has a problem, he turns to the ethics officer of the company. Dornseif has no work council yet; instead, the company's management proposed the ethics officer for the employees to turn to when needed.

The ethics officer received the confidentiality rights and obligations, so his colleagues can talk to him in a trustful atmosphere. »Back then, I needed the help of the ethics officer,« Ralf Stückenschneider recalls. »I had a problem I would not have taken straight to the boss.«

When Markus Dornseif moved to Münster with his wife in 2001, the couple started their own business – a company for facility management. They received an order from the British forces for snow removal. »As far as snow removal goes, we came to it like the Virgin to the child,« Markus Dornseif recalls. While there is a winter service at every place in Germany, there is no company that covers the entire spectrum.

After two years in business, Dornseif recognised they would occupy a certain niche with a Germany-wide offer. They positioned themselves strategically. In 2005, the couple acquired orders from all over Germany. Instead of letting the jobs be run by their own staff, they were painstakingly looking for network partners for the operational implementation on-site. By now, they have thousands of partners under contract; if one happens not to be available, another one can quickly pick up the work. The network must be large enough to operate redundantly. »If [the nationwide coffee shop chain] Tchibo previously needed winter service for all stores, they had to contract many local businesses,« explains Markus Dornseif. »Today, it is much easier. With us, our customers have only one contact partner. We take care of the rest. With our network partners, we always have someone who can go where the snow falls.« Dornseif, as central contact, takes care of the training, the planning, and the quality management. He is the only and central biller for the customer.

Katharina Gisbrecht is among Dornseif's long-time employees. »I still remember the early days,« says the young HR manager. »I came to my interview when the company was still in the old building. I thought to myself, ›What kind of association is that?‹ Because, back then, the first network partners waiting for a deployment were tough guys with many tattoos. However, I liked my conversation with Mr. Dornseif, and after one week, I realised this was the best decision of my life.«

In 2009, a major potential customer of Dornseif asked for a certification. Otherwise, the company would not be accepted as a service provider. »Therefore, I looked into ISO 9001, the quality management standard,« says Markus Dornseif. »And since I was already doing that, I also looked at ISO 14001 – environmental management – and ISO 18001 – protection of labour. It occurred to me: Everything you need for all these certifications, we already do.« The company lived much of what other companies are still working towards; it just needed to be documented and certified! For the certificate »Work and Family«, Dornseif could, for example, come up with the »Home-Office Kit.« If someone in the family falls ill, the employee can stay home and take care of the sick family member. »However, we define the family concept a little wider than others do,« says Markus Dornseif. »If an employee lives in an apartment and the roommate is sick, for us, that counts as family as well. Usually, one is not busy caring for the sick person around the clock. I know that from looking after my sick mother. There is still a lot of idle time.« That is when the »Home-Office Kit« comes into play. It enables employees to stay home and get paid relatively easily, while working during the employee's free time. The case is filled with a laptop, a high-speed mobile internet card, a small printer, and countless other tools for the desk at home. You can even get the suitcase delivered to your home. »My cat had to have surgery,« Jenny Kalbitz tells me. »I did not really have to care for her, but I felt more comfortable to be around her, so I asked how far the term ›extended family‹ can be stretched, and then I was able to work from home with the ›Home-Office Kit,‹« says the project manager.

If there is no child care available at short notice, employees can bring their children to work. Dornseif has invested much time and money in the safety of its employees: In fourteen years, there has not been a single industrial accident. Nevertheless, it is good to be prepared. For the children of employees, beside the »normal« first aid kit, there is a special first aid kit for children; after all, the worst pain often disappears more quickly with a colourful Band-Aid.

About this and other ways of cooperation, the company has reported to numerous auditors. Today, after several operational years, Dornseif has collected 16 different certificates, starting with the certificate »Work and Family« through »Age-appropriate Human Resource Development« to »Ethics in Business«, and not to forget all the relevant TÜV certified ISO standards. »You can't see those things separately,« Markus Dornseif thought, which created the impulse for employees and management alike to create, out of their already lived corporate culture, something of their own. They call it »Dreamwork.«

I get to know about this concept at 8:00 am, five minutes after entering the building. While I wait for the first business meetings, I watch the strongly gesticulating arms of Denise Blaschek. Actually, the management assistant only wanted to bring me a cup of green tea. However, since a two-by-two-meter-wide movable wall has been put up in the waiting room to describe the project Dreamwork, she explains it to me with enthusiasm and intense body language. »My colleague, Mrs. König, and I put it all in one linguistic and graphic mould,« she told me. »A lot of the project's content expresses who our colleagues and boss are. Basically, Dreamwork summarises the way we work together. It is the result of many years of jointly created corporate culture.« I ask Mrs. Blaschek why the corporate culture has to be summarised in writing. »Regularly, we introduce new employees, and with this written summary, we can more easily give them an overview on how we work, here.« Later, Markus Dornseif told me: »How should we, as dream bosses, dream employees behave in a dream company? That's what it is all about. Also, with Dreamwork, we can explain to other companies what exactly we do here.«

Differently from the Steigers, who found meaning through a traumatising event, the people at Dornseif found a strong positive anchor through Dreamwork. »That I am happy to go to work, for me, is Dreamwork,« says Ömer Tekin.

»Dreamwork is the reason colleagues, at peak times, when there is snow nationwide, sometimes, come to work even seven days a week,« says Katharina Gisbrecht. »That paves the way for dreamlike work results. However, that is only possible if the rest is also fantastic.« Magdalena Sroka, who manages customer service, adds: »For me, Dreamwork represents a special kind of humanity that is lived here. For us, it is now almost normal, but our customers tell us repeatedly that they feel this humanity when they visit us.«

The corporate culture bears effects. »The complaint rate is 0.4 per thousand,« says Markus Dornseif. »This is extremely low for the industry. If it really comes to be a problem, we have a whole team of people. This team ensures our local partner at site can solve the problem, or some other network partners can step in at short notice. Every year, we receive dozens of qualified reference letters.« The sickness rate in the 40-person company is only 1.3 percent, and the annual revenues have grown, since 2009, from 15 to 20 percent. »I believe the good results we all achieve here have a lot to do with the fact that management and employees always meet as equals,« says Ömer Tekin. »And the fact that we worked together to create the culture as it is today – this in itself, is a reason you like to go to work and give your best.«

After several discussions with the Dornseif staff, I finally meet Markus Dornseif. While walking to his office, I am tempted to expect a man with a blissful smile, a gentle handshake, and incense sticks. The opposite is the case. Instead of incense sticks, there are cigarettes, hence, the open window. He talks a lot, quickly, and forcefully. He is a loud, yet loveable, alpha leader, and he knows his effect on others. »Obelix fell into a cauldron of magic potion. For me, it was probably a bowl of speed,« he laughs when we talk about his personality. »Even my wife would say I have to slow down, and that, after meditating for 15 years,« says the 47-year-old father of three. In front of the open window, I spot a camp bed. »We make 10 million euro in sales in the course of the 40 days of the year when there is snow. In these peak periods, I need to be available around the clock.«

»Why this whole idea of Dreamwork? Why all this, which your employees so excitedly talk about?« I ask him at the end.

»Work is a part of life; these two things cannot be separated from one another,« he says. »I want the people around me to have a good life. Therefore, we have jointly created a work environment that, after all these years, we have put together under the name Dreamwork.«

However, he not only lives this concept at the company. It has happened in the past he has bailed out his employees from the police at 6:00 am, because they did not pay their tax bills. He pays his apprentices 20 percent more than usual, because »they cannot live on less.« An employee asking for a 50-euro salary advance for petrol from the HR manager on Friday receives 150 euro and a company car for the weekend.

»Intuitively, I believe everything we do here is also good for the company. However, I do not intend to measure what individual actions do.« In a recent anonymous external employee opinion survey for a certificate, staff delivered another result of what Dreamwork is about: 100 percent of the people interviewed said they would recommend their employer, without hesitation. »That,« an external auditor said later, »has never happened before in any company.«

Co-creation and meaningfulness

The company Dornseif employs a highly motivated and loyal workforce that works in an extraordinary culture. Noteworthy, though, is that this aspect of meaningfulness was not taught, but was deliberately created by all employees. The Dreamwork project results from a high amount of joint design, which in every company, should be experienced hand in hand with meaningfulness. If a manager encourages his staff to develop the company's strategy, but rejects the results afterwards, his staff will wonder why they bothered in the first place. The boss would fail if he tried a second time to engage his staff so fervently in such a process. The managing director of the government-related organisation in chapter 3 committed this grave error. If you enable a climate for people to shape their environment, it must also show a noticeable effect and lead to change. This happened at Dornseif in an exemplary manner. The Dreamwork project is, for everyone involved, a visible and tangible result of joint efforts. »My colleague, Mrs. König, and I put it all in one linguistic and graphic mould,« Denise Blaschek said. »When speaking of content, there is a lot that came from our colleagues in this project.« Why the Dornseif staff experienced such meaningfulness, I will demonstrate with the following experiments.

Man's search for meaning

If you believe a CEO like Joachim Weckmann or Markus Dornseif is always needed for meaningfulness in a company to take hold, I can encourage you: Even without a CSR or a Dreamwork strategy, executives can make a difference. Also, you do not need to be the owner or CEO of the enterprise for your staff to experience meaningfulness. It is simple ...

Do you remember the Ikea experiment from chapter 3? It was about the investigation in which the participants were prepared to pay more money for the same product than were the control group, only because they had previously put together the product on their own. In 2008, Dan Ariely, one of the senior scientists of this experiment, explored the influence of meaningfulness on our performance.

Ariely and his colleagues deliberately kept the, often very philosophically treated, meaningfulness simple. »We propose these twin factors (recognition and purpose) are two of the hidden motivational foundations of meaning-in-labour,« said the researchers at the beginning of their study. To uphold this hypothesis, they conducted two simple, yet very enlightening, experiments.

Imagine I give you a sheet of paper filled with disjointed letters. Somewhere between dozens of characters, I hide ten letter pairs, for example, two L (LL), two P (PP), or a pair of the remaining letters of the alphabet. I now ask you to find and underline these ten pairs. After you have done that and handed the paper back to me, I give you another sheet, which is also filled with letters. For the first processed sheet, you get 55 cents, for the second 50 cents, and 45 cents for the third. That would go linearly down to the 11th sheet, for which you only get five cents. From the 12th sheet on, there is no money to get anymore. »Our intention is to compare situations with no meaning (or as low a level of meaning as we can create),« Ariely says. The decisive and meaningful part of the experiment is as follows: Imagine two of your colleagues or friends also take part in this experiment. Both receive the same task. The only difference would be that you are to write your name on your sheet and hand it over to me directly. I will briefly look at your work and file it neatly before I give you another sheet.

Your first colleague will deliberately be asked not to write his name on the sheet. When he wants to hand in his results, with my head, I point to a stack of paper, saying: »Just put it over there.« Then he receives a new sheet for processing. Your second colleague will have a particularly memorable experience, now. He, too, is deliberately asked not to write his name on the paper. However, when he hands his results to me, without even looking at it and right in front of him, I put it through a shredder.

Consider your colleagues could quickly earn the maximum amount in this experiment. The result of their work is not checked and, in the case of the shredding, it wouldn't even be possible. Now, you needed only to put 10 strokes on your sheet of paper and hand it over to me, and you would receive the respective money. It would be 11 quick cycles. If I carefully check the results of your work, you are the only one of the three participants who has to deliver excellent work.

The result of the experiment turned out differently than many would expect. In Ariely's attempt, not three, but over 100 participants were divided into three equal groups. Group one, just as you, experienced ›recognition.‹ Group two experienced ›ignorance‹, and group three experienced ›shredding.‹ Each of the over 100 participants who participated in the experiment participated on their own, so they could not influence each other with their behaviour. Forty-nine percent of group one participants would go through all 11 cycles until there was no more money paid. One participant went through a 12th, unpaid cycle. Participants in the third group, who experienced the shredding, had less interest in performing the tasks. Only a meagre 17 percent of them – or about one-third as compared to group one – stuck it out for all 11 cycles. Not even the possibility of cheating was a good enough reason for the remaining 83 percent to make a quick buck and go through all 11 cycles. The scientists assumed, because shredding the work is such blatant, unnatural disregard for their results, this group would show the strongest reactions. They were wrong. The second group (»Do not write your name on the sheet, and place it simply on the stack of paper«), whose work results were ignored, reacted just as strongly as did the group with the shredding experience. Here, again, only 17 percent made it through all 11 cycles. To the great surprise of the scientists, none of the participants of the ›ignorance‹ group tried to cheat – Ariely and his team examined all the sheets afterwards.

> The realisation: Giving staff recognition will triple motivation. However, if you ignore people and their work results, it will demotivate the employees just as much as if you immediately destroyed their work efforts.

At Märkisches Landbrot, you can find a pronounced example of »recognition.« The numerous groups of visitors and media representatives, who watch the bakers at work, meet this need. In our conversation, Managing Director Weckmann summed it up: »For us, it is a form of respect that so many people want to see what we are doing here. It is an appreciation for what we stand for, for decades now.«

In another experiment, Ariely could confirm the influence of meaningfulness to commitment. However, he also came to two more insights. The newly recruited participants were divided into two groups. Each of them was given the task to build so-called Lego »Bionicles« out of 40 parts – small fantasy figures from the game manufacturer. For the first of these figures, the participants received $ 2, for the second $ 1.89, and $ 1.78 for the third – you already know the linear pattern from the experiment with the pairs of letters on a sheet of paper. The difference between the two experimental groups was that, while group one had an indefinite number of cardboard boxes with Bionicles available, group two got only two of those boxes. The investigators of group two would take those Bionicles apart, while the participant would put it back together again. In group one, which Ariely called the »meaningful group«, the participants were able to provide an ever-growing number of finished Bionicles on the table before them. The participants of group two, which Ariely called the »Sisyphus group«, had to watch how the results of their work were immediately torn apart again.

However, the researchers also recruited a third group that did not have to build Bionicles. Ariely told them about the test set up for group one and two and asked them for their assessment of how the participants of group one and two would behave. The surveyed participants of group three were unanimous: The meaningful group would assemble more Bionicles than the Sisyphus group, whose work product was destroyed. Group three believed the participants of the meaningful group, on average, would build one Bionicle more than the Sisyphus group.

How do you feel about it? What do you think? What measurable difference do you suspect between these two groups? »The surveyed participants tended to think in the right direction,« says Ariely. »But they completely underestimated the extent of their assumption.« Indeed, the meaningful group assembled more Bionicles than the Sisyphus group (whose figures were taken apart, while they assembled new ones at the same time). However, the difference was not only one figure on average, but four! The meaningful group had assembled an average of 11 Bionicles before the participants lost interest. Therefore, the measurable difference from the Sisyphus group was 47 percent. The work was the same; the pay was the same. The only difference was that the Sisyphus group realised the work fulfilled no purpose.

At Dornseif, staff realised through their Dreamwork Project, that their ideas were not discarded or destroyed. The joint work of the Dornseif employees to create this corporate culture led to a visible result: The Dreamwork project. The result is a high level of willingness to perform, similar to what could be observed by Ariely in his meaningful group. »Dreamwork is the reason colleagues, at peak times when there is snow nationwide, sometimes even come to work seven days a week,« says Dornseif employee Katharina Gisbrecht.

Ariely and his colleagues asked participants the following question: »Which one of you loves Lego?« They compared their answers with the test results and found there was a direct link between the »love of Lego« and the number of Bionicles built. The more participants indicated that they loved Lego, the more Bionicles the group built. However, this was only for participants of the meaningful group. For the Sisyphus group, the love of Lego did not affect their performance.

> Here, you can see Dan Ariely explaining his experiment: leading-brain.com/ariely

> Ariely's realisation through the experiment: »We are able to destroy the existing joy of something if employees can't find meaningfulness in what they do.«

Essence for Executives

Meaningfulness – People get access to their own resources

- If people find meaningfulness in what they do, it is easier for them to cope with challenging framework conditions.
- For decades, a married couple revolutionised the entire German emergency rescue system even though they experienced massive opposition. The avoidable death of their son is the force that drives them to overcome all obstacles.
- Deep within us, we carry the need to contribute. This can be observed in an infant: The child is happy to receive candies. However, it is measurably happier if it can give a portion of it to somebody else.
- If an employee knows of the CSR measures (and the positive impact on society) of its employer, they change their behaviour. They show a

measurably higher willingness to help colleagues, make frequent constructive proposals, and report less fatigue than those without CSR awareness.

- A study was undertaken in a company in which employees, for only one time, experienced 10 minutes of »meaningful impulses.« Their motivation increased by 142 percent, while their results increased a staggering 171 percent.
- According to a well-known study, giving an employee recognition for his work will increase his perceived meaningfulness and increase his motivation by a factor of three.
- If people lose faith in the meaningfulness of what they are doing, this may destroy even their previously existing interest and enthusiasm.

Chapter 7

Mindfulness –
People finding themselves again

>I came up with ideas, which I did not have before in such clarity.«

Heribert Gathof, CEO, Eckes-Granini Germany, 2000–2014

>My left arm felt like it was on fire,« said Mark Bertolini. He is tormented by spinal cord injury and neuropathy – a particularly troublesome form of pain, caused by direct damage to nerve tissue. >It never ceases. I can feel it even now,« he adds. Bertolini is chairman and CEO of Aetna, a US health insurer with 46 million customers and an annual turnover of EUR 58 billion. His odyssey of pain started in the mountains in 2004, following a skiing accident that broke his neck. He was lucky; by now, all his movements are almost back to normal. However, the severe spinal injury left his left arm in almost unbearable pain, Bertolini says. >At the beginning, I had to take up to seven different medications to keep the pain at bay,« he recalls. >Some of them were narcotics. While on those drugs, work was impossible for me.« The doctors advised him to accept the money from the disability insurance, to stay at home, and take high doses of medication for the rest of his life. However, for good reason, Bertolini did not listen to them.

A few years before this incident, Bertolini had second-guessed the statements of physicians and saved the life of his son, Eric. In 2001, Eric was diagnosed with incurable terminal cancer. Mark Bertolini suspended his job for 18 months and fought his way through the American healthcare system. The doctors gave Bertolini's son not more than six months. >So far, no one has conquered this form of cancer,« Bertolini says, remembering the physicians' statements. That Eric is alive today stems from Mark's persistence. He found a combination of life-saving therapies. >To date,

Eric is the only person I know who has survived this type of cancer,« says his father. »However, his kidneys have been destroyed by the treatment. That is why I donated my left kidney to him.«

When Mark Bertolini was, once again, tested by life, he chose a path free from pain and narcotics. He wanted to work again. Because he did not expect useful help from conventional medicine, he engaged in alternative healing methods.

»These days, I get up every morning at 5:30 to meditate,« says the CEO. »Asanas, pranayama, and vedic chants help me calm my mind and prepare for the mindfulness meditation. That's when I can sit down and go on my internal quest.« The elements of Hindu and Buddhist teachings are part of his »cocktail«: That's what Bertolini calls the mixture of methods, which enables him to deal with his neuropathy. »Craniosacral therapy, acupuncture, mindfulness, and yoga help me live without painkillers,« he says in a relaxed voice.

Inspired by his personal experiences, Bertolini made yoga and mindfulness accessible to all Aetna's 48,000 employees. To convince his management team of their effectiveness, he financed a research project that examined the impact of these methods on people in the workplace. »I did not want my team to think that, just because Mark is into yoga, everybody else has to do the same. The analysis of our workforce showed clearly that the top 20 percent employees, those who feel personal stress the most, have, per person, an average of $2,000 more medical costs than employees in the lowest fifth of the stress scale,« says Bertolini. In 2010, the company-sponsored research project began at Duke University. Two hundred and thirty-nine Aetna employees volunteered to participate in the study. Ninety of them were allocated to a yoga program. Ninety-six employees completed a specially designed awareness program for people in the working environment, called »Mindfulness at Work.« The remaining 53 employees were the control group.

The yoga program comprised 12 individual lessons in 12 weeks, while the mindfulness training comprised 14 hours in the same period. Research Director Ruth Wolever of Duke University and her team examined the subjectively mentioned and objectively measurable changes. »We found statistically significant improvements of personal stress and in the quality of sleep,« the scientist wrote in her study, published in 2012. She also found »significant improvement in heart rate variability« in the participants of the yoga and mindfulness courses. This is the ability of the heart to adapt quickly to different challenges, like sports or rest.

The management of Aetna analysed the change in the economic indicators. »We observed that the participants of the yoga and mindfulness courses had 62 minutes« more productivity after their classes,« said Bertolini. »This is a productivity gain of 3,000 dollars a year. Now, we make this program available to all Aetna employees.« Already, 13,000 of them have participated. The annual arithmetical productivity gain of Aetna amounts to 39 million dollars. Add to this the reduced medical costs per year. »In most cases, Aetna carried 80 percent of these costs,« Ruth Wolever told me. »These are the typical arrangements in the United States. In the beginning, Aetna offered the yoga and mindfulness courses in off-peak times, very early in the morning or in the evening. However, staff wanted 55-minute offerings during their lunch break, as well,« says Wolever. »These are the most popular courses.« Those lunch break courses are easier for staff to integrate into their day; at the same time, they feel the direct impact on their daily work.

While staff had to be present at the yoga classes, Aetna tested the mindfulness courses using two methods:

Participants could attend a course or log into an online course through their computer. The online courses comprised the live streaming of an instructor, who spoke in real time with all the participants online. Those online courses showed the same positive changes in personal feeling and productivity among participants as did the courses requiring physical presence. Some values, such as the reduction of perceived physical pain, showed greater improvement among those participating in the online course. »These days, almost all courses are exclusively offered online,« Elisha Goldstein told me. He has developed the »Mindfulness at Work« program and is one of several teachers, who performs the online courses.

»Many mindfulness training exercises include yoga elements. Are they implemented in the online courses, as well?« I asked.

»Yes. And the participants love to get out of their unhealthy office positions,« he says. »There are exercises where people rotate the upper body in front of their laptop or loosen the fingers with which they otherwise only type all day.«

Goldstein worked for various telecom companies in the dot-com years of the millennium. However, he turned his back on this part of his life, earned a doctorate in psychology, and has written several books on mindfulness. »By now, Aetna has released a lot of interesting indicators on the impact of mindfulness on the workforce. But how is the immediate feedback from the participants?« I ask Goldstein.

Company: Aetna Inc.
Industry: Health insurers
Headquarters: Hartford, Connecticut, USA
Established: 1853
Employees: 48,000
Website: www.aetna.com
Noteworthy: Over 13,000 employees participated in Yoga and Mindfulness courses. Besides the subjectively reported improvements in quality of life of the participants, CEO and Chairman Mark Bertolini estimates a cumulative productivity gain of those employees of over 30 million dollars.

»The feedback I get most from participants is, ›I have control over myself and my life again,‹« he replies. Christine Beaird, sales support consultant at Aetna, confirms this. Some years ago, the 44-year-old employee lost her husband. She drowned in sadness and depression and ate too much. »It has made such a huge difference in my life. I truly recommend it to anybody,« she says. »I have a better understanding of myself, my thought processes. This helped me feel more in control of my life.« Her colleague, Kellie Gregg, has been with Aetna for 34 years. She works from home and took part in the online mindfulness courses. »I work at home, tons of hours a day. I was just becoming very stressed,« she says. »By about the third week, I'm like, ›This is great. I'm sleeping better, I'm less stressed.‹ Now I manage my work much better; I learned how to turn away, just breathe, and that I can come back and focus. I'm much more productive.«

»Soon, Aetna will go one step further to provide more special mobile offers,« Ruth Wolever told me. »With smartphones and headphones in the ears, you can log into the live offerings, even when you are not at home or in the office.«

However, after the end of the 12-week course, most participants opted to practice the »formal« part of the mindfulness exercises alone, not during the lunch break, but early in the morning or in the evening. The »informal« part they repeatedly practice during the day. The Aetna Mindfulness at Work Program, which was originally developed by Goldstein, is now implemented by the provider eMindfulness and is available to employees from other organisations. Recently, the US state of Arizona offered the program to its 62,000 employees.

»My personal journey also influenced Aetna's ›Organisational Wellness‹,« says Bertolini. »The development of yoga and mindfulness at Aetna has my full support.« This development has become a ›heart issue‹ for Bertolini. In a conversation with journalists, I found him, as usual, to be restrained and controlled in all strategic corporate issues. When you ask about his mindfulness program, you experience a different Bertolini. He shows a more relaxed posture and talks animatedly. Those are the moments when the still chunky-looking Bertolini likes to talk about the 48 pounds he has lost and that he even recommended his doctor lose weight. To ensure mindfulness is not just lived in the 12-week program, but also implemented as a structural part of the management culture, Bertolini has adjusted the payment of his managers. Fifty percent of their salary now depends on how the bosses treat their employees. »You cannot behave like a jerk and expect to get paid,« Bertolini says, summarising the compensation system

A wandering mind

Imagine a glass filled with water. Then imagine you add two or three teaspoons of sand to the glass and stir. If, in your imagination, you got close to the glass of water, trying to look through it, what would happen? Due to the constant agitation, the sand would swirl, and the water would be cloudy. This represents the minds of most people in their normal state. Just like the sand in the tumbler, your thoughts are constantly swirling through your head. If you are not aware of this, by now, do a little experiment: When you reach the end of the sentence, stop reading. Instead, take 10 deep breaths and try to pay attention solely to your breath.

Most untrained people fail in keeping their mind focused on only one thing, even if it is only for the length of ten breaths. Automatically, our thoughts wander into the past (»What did my colleague mean earlier when he said ...«) or into the future (»I have to remember to buy asparagus ...«).

Many scientific papers have dealt with the wandering mind. In the 80 years from 1920 to 1999, 25 articles were written on this topic. In the years 2000 to 2013, interest skyrocketed. In those 13 years alone, 355 scientific articles were published. For a large part of our waking hours, we are elsewhere in our minds. Since the invention of smartphones, you can observe this phenomenon. How often have you seen others checking their phone regularly, even though no new messages have arrived? In 2010, researchers Matthew Killingsworth and Daniel Gilbert of Harvard University published a study of 5,000 people from 83 countries. Before the study, the participants downloaded to their iPhones an app that asked them several times a day about their well-being (On a scale of 0 to 100: How happy are you, right now?), their thoughts (Are you thinking of anything other than what you are doing, right now?) and their activities. A certain paradox cannot be denied: The scientists used those small devices, which constantly distract us, to find out if the subjects were distracted.

In 47 percent of the polled moments, participants admitted they were somewhere else with their thoughts. For example, they had a delicious dish in front of them and were thinking of something else. The only major exception was sex. This was the one matter for which participants had it all together ... At least until the Killingsworth and Gilbert iPhone app beeped, wanting to know what they were doing right then.

However, the more often participants clicked on the app while vacantly minded, the lower their average scores were on the happiness scale, even if they stated they had been busy with pleasant thoughts. The scientists evaluated the data over a longer period and came to the realisation:

The realisation: We do not wander with our thoughts because we are unhappy. The opposite is true: The constant wandering makes us unhappy!

Once again, imagine the glass of water in front of you. What would happen if you stopped to stir it? Slowly, the sand would sink to the bottom and the water would be clear. That would be your mind in a state of mindfulness when fewer thoughts are swirling through your head. If you keep your mind focused on 10 breaths, you give your mind a chance »for the sand to sink.« However, that does not mean you should try hard. It's about an inner »settling down« of your breath.

»Many people use the word ›mindfulness‹ erroneously as synonymous with the word ›attention,‹« Lienhard Valentin told me. Valentin is one of those avant-garde people in Germany who have been practicing mindfulness for the last 25 years. Through his small publishing company Arbor, Valentin regularly publishes German and international literature on the subject. »Mindfulness is a very special form of attention. It is more like a benevolent, non-judgmental presence in the here and now, an openness to our present experience,« says Valentin.

If I were to ask you again to focus totally on your breathing (so the sand in your mind can sink), you would probably feel physical sensations or thoughts and emotions would emerge in your consciousness. What usually happens: We get carried away by all those stories and impulses. Subsequently, we lose our focus on the moment and our breath. The methodology described by Valentin as »non-judgmental« means we perceive body, thoughts, and emotions solely, without putting these experiences in a box and judging them as pleasant or unpleasant. For example, you feel some kind of sensation, and your immediate thought (carrying you away from the moment) might be: »I need to make an appointment for a massage.« A value-free approach would look like this: »Interestingly, I feel a twinge in my back. How does that feel exactly? Can I open myself to the sensation? Explore it?« However, if you then think, »I need to call my boss,« a natural consequential thought might be: »How do I convince him that ...?« Already, and without thinking, you are caught up in a story that has nothing to do with the here and now. If you practice mindfulness, you watch the thoughts only briefly and without appraisal (»Interestingly, I thought of my boss!«). Then you come back to your breath again.

Every person can do this. What makes us different is the time we can spend in such a mindful state. For the untrained mind, this mindful state can last less than a second, but everybody can learn it.

The training of mindfulness is separated into a formal and informal practice. The formal practice is, for example, the one laid out here by me: Sit down in a quiet place, focus on your breath, and make sure your mind cannot be carried away by bodily sensations, emotions, or thoughts. These exercises are practiced by Aetna CEO Mark Bertolini every morning and by many of his employees during their lunch sessions. With this formal practice, you train your mind and build new neural networks in your brain, which eventually will help you stay longer in this mindful state.

The rest of the day, you can practice formless mindfulness by stopping yourself every now and then and asking yourself: Am I in the here and now, or in mind was I elsewhere? The objective of the informal practice of mindfulness is to get yourself back into the present moment and bring your wandering mind back.

»Although mindfulness techniques have been around for thousands of years, and even though methods, such as MBSR (Mindfulness-Based Stress Reduction), have been developed for the western world as easy-to-learn techniques over the last decades,« says Lienhard Valentin, »the subject only gained popularity through the findings of modern brain research.«

The Neuroscience of mindfulness

Do you remember the visit the Dalai Lama made to the American neuro-science laboratories from chapter 1? During a demonstration of technical equipment, one participant moved his finger; soon after, the brain scanner showed an activation of the associated motor network in his brain. The Dalai Lama asked the man to move his fingers only in his mind. As the participant did as he was asked, the brain scanner showed an activation of the same motor network. »Our thoughts affect the activity of the brain,« the Dalai Lama recognised at that time. This was an important moment, because with his own eyes, he watched the scientific evidence for something that Buddhists have believed all along: Our thoughts can influence our bodies, in this case, our brains.

The researcher who carried out those experiments in his laboratory at the University of Wisconsin in Madison, during the visit of His Holiness in 2001, was Richard Davidson. Today, he is regarded as one of the world's most famous brain researchers. He reached his popularity partly through his cooperation with the Dalai Lama and his research with Buddhist monks. The specific characteristic of his research are that Davidson could show a never-before-seen activity within the brains of these monks.

However, his research had had quite a bumpy start, had been very costly, and absolutely fruitless. In 1992, Davidson put together all his courage and wrote a letter to the Dalai Lama to ask for help. The Tibetan leader was already living in his Indian exile in Dharamsala. In the mountainous region around the new home of His Holiness, dozens of meditating monks had been living a life of solitude for many years. Davidson wanted to study the effects of years of meditation. Therefore, he asked the Dalai Lama to put in a good word for him and his investigations. He found open ears; His Holiness has always been very receptive towards the Western sciences. If you have seen the film *Seven Years in Tibet*, about the life of the Austrian Heinrich Harrer (played by Brad Pitt), you know the Dalai Lama likes to engage with technical matters. »Most likely, I would have become an engineer, but then the whole thing about the reincarnation of the previous Dalai Lama got in the way,« he jokes.

With respect to Richard Davidson's concern, he asked his intermediary to contact the meditating men in the mountains and tell them about the Dalai Lama's request that they be examined by a western scientist. Ten monks agreed. Davidson went to Dharamsala with his colleagues Cliff Saron, Francisco Valera, and Allan Wallace. They had several tons of technical equipment and a research budget of $ 120,000– and they returned empty-handed. Even though he succeeded, with the help of local volunteers, in getting 420 pounds of his most important equipment across the mountain paths to visit those men, one by one, he was not able to convince even one monk to engage in his scientific research. Most likely, they agreed at the beginning only because the Dalai Lama had requested it of them. Some of the common answers he received were that their progress in meditation was not yet sufficient to create any remarkable results. Humility is one of the highest Tibetan virtues. However, this virtue spelled the undoing for the scientists' case. When the arduous journey ended, the dejected Davidson received the Dalai Lama's promise he would look for monks who would come to the laboratories in Wisconsin.

The incident described in chapter 1 was this promise; it had taken nine years, but in May 2001, the Dalai Lama and a close confidant visited the laboratory of Richard Davidson in Wisconsin. This confidant was a former French scientist, Matthieu Ricard, who already as a young man had exchanged his worldly life for life as a monk in the Himalayas, close to the Dalai Lama. The encounter between Ricard and Davidson was the beginning of a long, fruitful cooperation that would not only leave its marks on the world of science, but that also extended to the economy. In 2014, 13 years after their first meeting, both were sought-after participants in the World Economic Forum in Davos.

In the media, Ricard is often referred to as »the happiest man in the world«, because Davidson shows high activity in the part of the brain responsible for personal well-being.

In particular, the left prefrontal cortex (PFC) of Ricard showed unusually high activity. In the 1980s, Davidson had, in several experiments, shown with the simplest of instruments increased activity in the left PFC, which can be associated with pleasant feelings. Increased activity in the right PFC, however, is associated with the sensation of unpleasant feelings.

In 1986, Davidson published a research report in which he demonstrated the neural connections exist in newborns. In his experiment, he put a little sugar water on the lips of two- to three-day-old babies. Tiny electrodes from his measuring instruments attached to the infants' scalps showed a significant increase in activity in the left PFC. If he put lemon water on the infants' lips, the activity of the left PFC shifted to the right.

Here, you can see Matthieu Ricard talking about »happiness«: leading-brain.com/ricard

In 1982, in less »invasive« experiments, Davidson reached the same results. Ten-month-old babies who saw enjoyable video clips with laughing people showed the same left-sided activation of the PFC as did the new-borns who got sugar water on their lips. However, if the babies saw a video clip of a crying woman, their prefrontal activity would shift from the left to the right, as was the case with the babies who got lemon water on their lips.

Buddhist monk Matthieu Ricard, who, through regular meditation, has a highly active left PFC, regards his nickname »the happiest man in the world« as flattering. However, he is quick to point out that only a small part of mankind has had such elaborate investigations, with methods such as Davidson's, applied to it. At the same time, Ricard, a former scientist, knew about the necessity of underpinning Davidson's initial research with research on additional monks. Therefore, he helped Davidson find monks willing to take part in his scientific studies. After 18 months, Davidson was able to examine, in his laboratories, eight monks who had 10,000 to 50,000 hours of meditation experience. They were also champions of mindfulness meditation. When he finally published the results of his work in 2004, Davidson wrote: »We demonstrated a stronger gamma activity in all monks. Higher than it was ever documented in the scientific literature.«

If you put one of these EEGs (networks of 256 electrodes by which scientists measure the activity of brains) on people like you and me, you would probably find only a small gamma wave, occasionally. Gamma waves occur when people are very concentrated and focused on an action. This gamma wave can also be seen briefly in those fleeting »moments of insight« of which we will talk later. These waves are momentary. When such a wave emerges, it disappears quickly. In those monks whom Davidson could investigate, the gamma waves were not just constantly visible; they were 30 times more intense than within people like us. Thousands of hours of meditation had measurably changed the way the brains of these monks worked.

Parallel to his studies with the monks, Davidson wanted to know what impact meditation would have on people with no mindfulness experience. In 1999, he started a joint study with the most important Western protagonist in mindfulness meditation: Jon Kabat-Zinn. Kabat-Zinn, a molecular biologist, developed in 1979 a method called MBSR (»Mindfulness-Based Stress Reduction«). This method implemented, among other things, elements of Buddhist Vipassana, Zen, and Hindu Yoga. He deliberately excluded the spiritual overtone of the old oriental knowledge to make MBSR easily accessible for Westerners. MBSR has been used as a form of therapy in some US hospitals to help people with stress-related pathologies. Due to its high efficacy, doctors recommend this mindfulness method because of its outstanding results among people with chronic pain, eating disorders, and a variety of other mental and physical disorders. Gustav Dobos, head of the Department of Naturopathy and Integrative Medicine at the Clinic Essen-Mitte, gets to the point about the effect of MBSR: »If we could achieve such effects as with MBSR with medication, it would be medical malpractice not to use this method.«

Jon Kabat-Zinn was thrilled that a neuroscientist wanted to examine his, to many thousands of people, successfully applied method. Although there were already a few qualified MBSR teachers, Kabat-Zinn took it upon himself to teach MBSR to Davidson's selected participants. The classic MBSR course lasts eight weeks. Once a week, students meet for three hours to learn the method and how to apply it. The students are instructed to practice what they have learned for 30 to 45 minutes each day between their meetings. In addition, after the sixth week, an entire »Mindfulness Day« is performed. All this is the »formal« part of the program. The so-called »informal« part of the MBSR practice is applied by students throughout the day, without additional time re-quirements. For example, a student is asked to have one meal daily in a mindful manner (or perform any other activity in a mindful manner). Repeatedly, he stops what he is doing and checks in: »Am I in the here and now? Do I perceive what is happening? Or am I with my thoughts somewhere else?«

Davidson investigated several aspects of the participants. First, before and immediately after the eight-week course, he put the hairnet-like structure (EEG), with its hundreds of electrodes, on the students' heads to observe their brain activity. Four months after the training was finished, he examined their brains one more time. In addition, before and immedi-ately after the MBSR course, each participant was given a questionnaire to document their subjective feelings about anxiety and stress. Because the end of the course coincided with the start of flu season, each participant received a flu shot. Blood samples were taken before and after the vac-cination, and Davidson investigated the number of antibodies produced by the vaccine. As with any study, a control group went through all the tests, but did not participate in the MBSR course.

The 2002 published study, called »Alterations in Brain and Immune Function Produced by the Mindfulness Meditation«, showed startling results: The anxiety symptoms, subjectively described by the participants, were reduced by 12 percent, while the production of antibodies as a result of the influenza vaccination was higher by five percent among the MBSR participants. Last, the activity of the left prefrontal cortex (PFC) had increased significantly. Among those students who participated in the MBSR course, the activity of the PFC was, after four months, still three times higher than it was at the beginning of the investigation.

The realisation: A regularly applied mindfulness practice changes the function of the human brain.

The higher activity could be compared to a road network, where suddenly, at peak times maybe, more cars are on the road. A new network would be comparable to widening the road or building a new one, so the traffic moves faster and more efficiently. To find out if mindfulness causes new networks (of the brain), the scientists needed another method to examine the participants. The results from Davidson, who used EEGs, were not sufficient for that. With an EGG, activation patterns and waves can be measured; therefore, it becomes apparent whether there is more activity in a particular part of the brain. However, structural changes due to neuro-plasticity (and new networks) are not detectable with an EEG. To detect those structural changes, so-called magnetic resonance imaging (MRI) was needed. Although Davidson had those devices in his laboratory, he used them only to examine the brains of the monks, who had accumulated 10,000 to 50,000 hours of meditation. However, what effects do mind-fulness exercises have on the brain structures of people like you and me?

The German psychologist Britta Hölzel can give us the answer through a study published in 2011. Hölzel conducted research for several years at the Harvard Medical School in Boston, and in this period, she mainly examined human brains using an MRI. She focused her studies on the changing brains of meditating people. There had already been cross-sectional studies that examined the differences in the neural structures of the brains of different people, for example, comparing monks with managers. The problem with cross-sectional studies, however, is that the brain of a monk could have already been structured differently before the 10,000 hours of meditation. Therefore, Hölzel carried out a longitudinal study: She wanted to know how much the structure of the brain of an average person changed through regular mindfulness practice.

Hölzel's studies are now frequently mentioned in the context of the Western MBSR method. She studied mindfulness and other traditional Hindu and Buddhist methods directly in India and Thailand. »Back then, I had not heard of the MBSR method,« she recalls. After her time in Boston and a year at the Charité in Berlin, I caught up with her in February 2015 at her parents' home in Munich. »After high school, I was in India for six months. More by ›accident‹, I ended up in a yoga ashram,« she tells me. »I was very excited about the experiences I had there. Unfortunately, this knowledge had no place in my subsequent study of psychology.«

However, when Britta Hölzel wrote her doctoral thesis, she could connect her experience professionally. At the Justus-Liebig University in Giessen, she met the psychologist and meditation researcher Ulrich Ott. »That's when I first came across MBSR,« she says. »The technique is very clear, but it lacks the spiritual side as I knew it from Asia. Jon Kabat-Zinn took on the Vipassana part in a strict sense, as I learned it in the Thai monastery.«

When Hölzel realised the effect of MBSR in the Western world, she wanted to understand precisely what effect this mindfulness method has on our brains. To do that, she went to Boston.

If you had never practiced MBSR or any other mindfulness technique, were right-handed, were aged between 25 and 55 years, and were on no medication, you were the ideal candidate for Britta Hölzel's study at the Massachusetts General Hospital. Relatively early in the study, Hölzel examined subjects with an MRI. Subjects participated in an eight-week MBSR course and then had their brains scanned a second time.

The essential and very encouraging results in advance: After these few weeks of mindfulness, Hölzel and her colleagues saw significant changes in the brains of the participants. The other, mindful way of thinking rewired regions of the brain, while other areas became smaller or, respectively, bigger at the same time.

»We could observe, in this and in other studies, that if a person applies regular mindfulness, there is an increase of the grey matter in the hippocampus,« says Britta Hölzel. »A decrease in the grey matter in certain areas of the amygdala was also observed, which came hand in hand with the reduction of the personally perceived stress levels of the participants.«

The realisation: Regular practice of mindfulness changes the structure of the human brain.

The hippocampus has several important functions in the brain. First, it is a kind of librarian: It »knows« in which neuronal structures it stores information and where it can retrieve this stored information. Thus, the hippocampus plays a central role in learning and memory processes. In addition, the hippocampus is the nerve cell factory of the brain: It produces new brain cells. If we experience a high level of personal stress, the hippocampus is one of the first neural structures affected. If there is a high level of stress, individual cell structures of the hippocampus die. Successively, it withdraws its connections to the other parts of the brain. Learning and memorising become increasingly difficult. The hippocampus also reduces the production of new brain cells, called neurogenesis. When the brain suddenly reproduces fewer new nerve cells, you do not have to be a scientist to understand this is not particularly good. People with depression or burnout symptoms often receive so-called selective serotonin reuptake inhibitors. These drugs act on the hippocampus similar to a regular mindfulness practice: It starts growing again.

The amygdala assumes the role of »danger detector.« When there is a real threat (a speeding car) or even a perceived risk (a rumour in the company of an upcoming reorganisation), it sounds an alarm. For most people in Western countries, the amygdala is activated by supposed, rather than real, dangers: We literally stress ourselves out. However, an amygdala scaled down through the practice of mindfulness is associated with less (homemade) stress. »In those examined people, the stress level dropped significantly,« Britta Hölzel explains.

Klosterfrau in mindfulness

»At a certain age, it's normal you have physical ailments – as I have high blood pressure and frequent headaches,« says Horst Inden. »At least, that's what I thought until, one day, I stood in a bookstore in front of Jon Kabat-Zinn's book. It was about health and meditation.« Inden is head of HR and education at Klosterfrau Vertriebsgesellschaft, the same section of the Klosterfrau Group, which became known by the very name *Klosterfrau Melissengeist* (a well-known German medicine based on a 400-year-old recipe). The medium-sized company is the market leader in the non-prescription drugs industry. It sells, among other brand names, the mosquito repellent *Autan* and the famous Swiss herbal candies *Ricola*.

»Back then, as a young adult, I trained in martial arts. At the beginning and end of the training, we always meditate for a few minutes, to focus. By recalling this time, Kabat-Zinn's book seemed familiar, so I bought it,« says Inden. It was his first contact with MBSR, the mindfulness method developed by Jon Kabat-Zinn.

Inspired by the book, Inden started with a regular mindfulness practice. »I was wrong to assume that pain and high blood pressure are just part of it,« he says today. »After some time, my symptoms improved. Even my friends and colleagues told me I was more focused and made better observations during discussions.« After Inden had experienced the effects of mindfulness on his own body and mind, he was eager to bring this method and inner attitude to the company, as well. »At first, I had a lot of concerns about how the employees would respond,« says the 52-year-old. »I expected a lot more reservations than there actually were.« During an organisational development process in 2006, Inden began to incorporate individual elements of mindfulness: He started with the general attitude of the management culture, based on the method of mindfulness. »For example, we agreed on certain rules on how to interact with each other, such as mutual respect, trust, fairness, team spirit, professionalism, and openness, without explicitly mentioning this had something to do with mindfulness.« Later, the company introduced the so-called »mindful project workshops,« which, in part, required the participants to spend a few minutes in silence on the days of the workshop. »I remember it was particularly hard for my boss to remain in silence. That was almost monotone. But at the end of the project meetings, he came to me, pleased with the results. This experience was unfamiliar for him at the beginning,« says Inden. »He could only partly identify with this exercise, but in his opinion, back then, the meeting for this project was a breakthrough.«

After the Klosterfrau workforce had shown a certain openness to mindfulness, Inden went one step further: In 2009, he employed an MBSR teacher to teach mindfulness on-site. »I also enlisted an external psychologist to develop questionnaires for the participants,« he says. »In the first year, we had participants fill out these questionnaires. I had the feeling that, somehow, I had to justify these measures and prove their effectiveness.« The answers to the questionnaires were compared to those of a control group. The result was very encouraging: Participants reported a better morning mood, were more energetic, more mentally alert, and less depressed than before. The commonly reported statement was that depression and burnout levels had decreased.

The acceptance of mindfulness courses quickly could be felt far beyond the questionnaires. »The fact we have a stress problem in our society, and therefore, in our company, is obvious to everyone in a key position,« says Inden. »They also understood quickly that mindfulness is a good way to deal with this.«

Inden remembers a key situation that occurred several years ago. Back then, a well-known consulting company put several external cost items of the company to the test. That practiced mindfulness is supportive of the workforce, the consultants did not question. The management was, in any event, supportive of this issue. »We have found there are many similarities between the practice of mindfulness and what is important to us when dealing with each other,« says Klosterfrau's head of HR. The result: The costs of the mindfulness courses were allocated under »health care.«

»Like most companies, we have to cope with the fact that employees drop out due to mental illness. Although our sick leave rate is 15 percent below the average of our industry, some things can't be avoided,« says Inden. »However, I made a remarkable observation. Not one employee who consistently participated in the MBSR courses has fallen ill to a mental illness, so far.«

Meanwhile, half the office staff of the Cologne distribution company has experience with mindfulness activities. »I think, as a workforce and a company, we are well on our way to changing our inner attitude,« says Inden. »The last employee survey showed that our employees have an above-average commitment to the company.«

Fast insight – slow thinking

Here is a little quiz with which to begin: Dr. Jung from Berlin has a brother in Munich, a notary. This notary, however, says: »I have no brother in Berlin who holds a doctor degree.« How can that be?

For some people, the solution is obvious. Others think for a moment, believing they won't find the answer; they feel blocked, until they have an epiphany. A third group might still be thinking.

If you were among the first two groups, you had an insight – you experienced that the solution was »suddenly« just there. Maybe you thought for a moment, without going through every cognitive step. People experience similar things when taking a shower or jogging or during other moments of mental relaxation. In these moments of mentally letting go, we have thoughts or ideas that are not as easily accessible during moments of everyday stress. Insight is a thought that would have taken longer through a cognitive derivation. Sometimes, you cannot derive it at all due to mental constructs. Such a blocking mental construct is the assumption that a »doctor« must be male. It obstructs the insight that Dr. Jung from Berlin is the sister, not the brother of the notary Jung in Munich.

By now, insights can be measured in the brain. Researchers Mark Beeman and John Kounios have been specialists in this field for more than a decade. What makes them so remarkable is that Beeman prefers to work with functional magnetic resonance imaging (fMRI), while Kounios prefers working with the EEG. With his fMRI, Beeman can accurately track where something changes in the brain. However, his method is a few seconds too slow to capture the rapid insight reaction of a participant. With the help of the EEG, Kounios can directly measure any change in the brain frequency, however inaccurate it might be. When both combined their results, they came to astonishing conclusions about the place and time of such an insight.

When I contacted Kounios to learn more about his work, he told me about the surprising test result with a Zen meditator who, in a scientific environment, achieved extraordinary insight results. Kounios' stories remind me of conversations with some of the business leaders who practiced mindfulness. Heribert Gathof, former CEO of Eckes-Granini Germany, is one. After four years of regularly practicing the mindfulness meditation, he can report: »It sounds paradoxical, in this quietness, this silence, this not-wanting-to-think, that ideas will emerge, that I did not have before, at least, not in this clarity.« Through regular mindful practice, Gathof has created necessary neuronal connections, so even in his everyday life, insight processes are easier.

From a neurobiological point of view, this insight process happens in two phases: In the preparatory phase, the executive functions of our prefrontal cortex (PFC) are active. They focus on the problem and reduce the activity of other cortical areas of the brain. While you were reading the riddle of Dr. Jung, your PFC automatically ensured some brain regions not required for problem solving quiet down temporarily. »To focus on something means to mask other things,« says Mark Beeman. In this preparatory phase of the insight process, areas of the cortex are slowed down, in particular, those which process our senses. »If we think of something, we close our eyes; the cortex does this for the same reason,« adds Beeman.

This is followed by the »seeking« phase of the insight process. The brain scans different neural networks to come up with a solution. In this phase, Beeman and Kounios were able to observe high activity in the neuronal networks responsible for speech and voice processing. In these moments, which can take a few seconds, some people might feel blocked: »I just can't get it right now. Just give me a moment.« You realise, basically, the solution is available. This is typical of an insight process. Do you remember when I asked you to focus on 10 breaths? And how quickly other thoughts came to your mind? For those who have already practiced mindfulness, to control those thought impulses will pay off any time they are entering the stage of an insight process. The better you have learned to focus, the easier it is for the PFC to scan those neural networks for solutions.

In those moments, Kounios can measure a high intensity of alpha waves with his EEG – a condition your brain will recognise from your mindfulness practice. However, at the moment of insight, the EEG picture changes dramatically: The alpha waves decrease rapidly and are replaced by sharply rising gamma waves. This is a clear sign there is a sudden large number of brain cells from the most remote areas of the cortex coming together to create a new, unprecedented network. The new idea is there! It is a neuronal manifestation.

Perhaps, you remember Richard Davidson detected a high intensity of gamma waves in the meditating monks. Kounios had a similar, most remarkable experience with a man who had trained his mind well. »In 2007, a man practicing Zen Meditation came to see me in my lab,« Kounios told me. The approximately 40-year-old man wanted to measure his brainwaves and wanted to know what effects all those years of meditation had on his brain. Kounios describes the encounter in great detail in his book, *The Eureka Factor*. He examined the brain of the meditator with his EEG and noted, »it was special.« After this simple test, there was some time left. The Zen meditator was curious about what else Kounios explored in his laboratory. Kounios offered to let him participate in some of the insight tests. He gave him the same tasks that dozens of volunteers had previously solved. The tasks were either cognitive (you have to think about them) or solved through insight (the answer suddenly appears).

Consider how you would solve this task: You get three words and need to find a fourth word, which connects those given words: humour, pitch, night.

The correct answer would be »black.« Did you cognitively match this or did the answer just »pop up?« Here is another set of words: bunny, cloud, colour.

Those tasks are from the Remote Associates Test, developed by Sarnoff Mednick in 1968. The correct answer would have been »white.«

In the beginning, the meditator in Kounios's laboratory could not find any insightful answers. His mind had been trained to suppress all thoughts. However, as soon as he realised he only had to let go of logical thinking, he suddenly solved dozens of tasks through insight. Kounios writes about the man trained in mindfulness: »Never before did we see anybody who could solve so many tasks just as quickly.«

Upstalsboom | Years of mindfulness

If you ask Lienhard Valentin, founder of the Arbor publishing house, which specialises in mindfulness to define the term »mindfulness«, you receive a precise formulation. I got to experience this precision myself.

Although I have been involved in mindfulness for several years, Valentin made comments about different terms in the part of this chapter I sent to him for checking his quotes before publishing. Two men involved with the same topic for years still have a linguistically different understanding of mindfulness.

Imagine what happens in many companies, whose employees aren't much into mindfulness for professional reasons. In dozens of workshops, I have seen how »mindfulness« found its way into parts of the code of conduct, guidelines, corporate values, or other directional constructs. When I ask the participants about their understanding of mindfulness, I get answers that do not reflect the actual meaning, but nonetheless point in the right direction: »Being more in the moment«, »being in touch with others«, »slowing down«, »working relationships«, and other similar interpretations. Many employees have their own ideas as to what mindfulness could be. At the same time, I experience how easily a consensus can be achieved in a company. If that is accomplished, the employees are usually very willing to adjust their own actions accordingly.

Even with the hotel chain Upstalsboom, the term »mindfulness« popped up during its mission statement workshop. »My employees painted a picture,« says Owner and Managing Director Bodo Janssen. »The picture depicted me as the engineer of an express train. Behind the express train drove a slow train with my employees.« Janssen is known for bringing new ideas to the company. »Mr. Janssen has the ability to think things through quickly,« says Head of HR Bernd Gaukler. »I know quite some managers who think equally fast; however, they underestimate the impact on the workforce at times. It happened here, as well, that employees suffered, at times, because new projects were continually initiated.« Because of the winds of change at Upstalsboom and the focus on »happy people,« staff has the courage to report such things to their boss. »We can't spend all our time in the future, Mr. Janssen,« the manager says, recalling the statements of his employees. »Every now and then, we want to be in the here and now and simply be proud of our achievements.« Therefore, the 70 participants of the workshop chose mindfulness as one of 12 corporate values of Upstalsboom. As with all the other values, there was a matching mindfulness slogan too: »We live for the moment and shape the future!« Bernd Gaukler adds: »In addition to, ›being in the moment,‹ many colleagues extended the value to how they deal with each other. This issue was so close to the heart for the Upstalsboom staff that in another workshop, 80 of them decided to make mindfulness a key corporate value for 2013.

»Just look at the Upstalsboom-Landhotel Friesland in Varel,« recommends Gaukler. »In this hotel, the value of mindfulness was very well-implemented.« The train ride from Oldenburg to Varel takes only 20 minutes. The taxi ride from the station to the hotel takes another 10 minutes. The Landhotel Friesland is built on a small, secluded lake. You can walk around it in only half an hour. Pure tranquillity.

»After the takeover, Hotel Director Marc Stickdorn faced disastrous conditions on several levels,« Gaukler says. »However, with his mindful attitude, he managed such that the formerly highly insecure employees now feel they are in good hands again.«

For example, before the previous owner led the house into bankruptcy, he sold large quantities of wellness vouchers. After re-opening by Upstalsboom, the voucher holders gathered on the doorstep to get the services they had purchased. »We're talking about a high six-figure sum, which the previous owner had not told us about and was now demanded by the customers,« Marc Stickdorn told me on a late Sunday evening.

The first months after the reopening, the infamous area manager (you read about him in chapter 5, the one who was subsequently dismissed by Bodo Janssen) led this hotel. Then Stickdorn moved from another Upstalsboom Hotel and took over the house in Varel. »I found two things,« says the man in his late forties. »A divided team that does not really work well together, and a planned sales growth which, in my opinion, was not achievable.« Stickdorn reviewed the figures closely and, eventually, corrected the expected profit downward by 500,000 euro. »I still remember it as if it were yesterday: It didn't even take two minutes after sending the email to have the head of controlling of our group on the phone. He thought I had made a mistake in one of the formulas. Unfortunately, I had to break it to him that my formula was right. However, the profit-promise of my predecessor was wrong.«

This was followed by 18 hard months. Both the first and the following financial year's hotel manager closed with a negative result.

For the staff, there was another challenge: dealing with each other. »We had three groups of employees. First, people who knew the hotel from the time of the previous owner, second, the neutral new ones, and third, the personal protégées of my predecessor, the area manager, who had led the hotel a few months,« says Stickdorn.

Stickdorn's personal opinion about the low-motivated and fragmented staff was confirmed after he received the results of a company-wide employee opinion survey shortly after taking over the hotel. The employee satisfaction level was a lean 40 percent. In the qualitative feedback, he read phrases like: »It lacks fairness«, »We do not feel any loyalty« and »We are not a team.« Bärbel Schramm, a long-standing commercial clerk, remembers: »The worst thing about the ›new colleagues‹ from Upstalsboom was they gave us old-timers the feeling that we couldn't do anything right and that we were also to blame for the bankruptcy. There was a very harsh tone, which often became personal. Either you were one of them and carried out instructions without questions, or you were threatened with dismissal. Power, pressure, and commands were commonplace!«

Marc Stickdorn asked Bernd Gaukler to help dissolve the »old boys' network« of his predecessor and lead the workforce to an action-enabled state over the coming months. »I knew the labour court judge by her first name,« he recalls of this stressful time.

»How did the rest of the staff respond after all those layoffs? Did it lead to more uncertainty?« I wanted to know from Stickdorn.

»On the contrary,« he replies. »Many perceived this as a liberation and relief.«

Bärbel Schramm told me later: »We were relieved, because the way we dealt with each other, suddenly everything was much more comfortable. It was human again, and immediately, we felt we and our work were valued. Even the reputation of the hotel improved, because we could focus on our work, once again.«

It would have been easy for Stickdorn to bring quick money into the house. With discounter chains, like Aldi or Lidl as partners, the industry can fill rooms well. »In my opinion, if we did that, we would have burnt out our staff,« he says. Although – or perhaps because – the hotel manager found himself in the middle of a storm, he put the brakes on a quick change. He decided, with Bodo Janssen, to pursue long-term gains and high quality, while accepting short-term losses.

»We need a different form of cooperation, to provide good long-term work and be profitable,« was Stickdorn's credo. »The employees were still unsettled; there was hardly any team spirit; everybody just did their job,« he says. »Even just the word, ›department‹ expressed the problem: People were ›departed‹ from each other. Therefore, I proposed speaking of ›workspaces‹ instead.«

Stickdorn put mindful dealing with each other at the top of his agenda. He started with simple, but effective, changes that determined the working environment on a day-to-day basis. For example, all »workspace« leaders would meet daily for five minutes to improve contact between all areas of the hotel. Kerstin Zingler, who runs the front office, told me: »In those short daily meetings, we can discuss the entire day and pay attention to special needs and moods.«

»Now, Mr Stickdorn treats us with dignity,« says Spa Director Kerstin Lehmann. Stickdorn is even a regular guest at all the workspace meetings. That gives each of his 70 employees the opportunity to get in touch with him in an informal way. Once a month there is a coffee meeting with Stickdorn, to which he invites all the staff members who had a birthday in the last month. »By now, the staff knows how important it is to me that we each maintain good relationships and that we pay attention to how everyone is feeling,« says the hotel manager. »Recently, we had a temporary staff member from another Upstalsboom house here with us. When she went back after 10 weeks, staff arranged a special breakfast for her. She was very touched and said she had never experienced anything like that – and that was after just 10 weeks.«

The employees of the country hotel (Landhotel) in Varel see themselves as the source of the mindfulness movement at Upstalsboom. Eighty participants from other houses and the headquarters met at the Stickdorn hotel to participate in a joint workshop, where they made mindfulness the most important value for the year 2013. »I believe that, through several conversations with the participants, much rubbed off onto other areas, so other employees, too, received those impulses,« Stickdorn muses.

The impact on the workforce is now measurable in black and white. The number of sick days and the turnover rate in Varel are the lowest in the Upstalsboom group. »It is obvious that employees treat each other differently, now,« says Stickdorn. »Recently, an employee from the front office came to see me. She and her colleague from the reception gave the bonus payment some thought.« While the front office had already received two bonus payments and a third one was pending, for the colleagues from room service a bonus payment wasn't even planned.« Reservations Manager Annika Warring told me: »We are a team, and we pull together. If the rooms are not cleaned, we cannot sell them. In my opinion, everybody needs to be involved.« Warring and her colleagues from the front desk offered to give up 50 percent of their bonus payment, so their colleagues from room service would get some, too.

The long way was worth it, not only on a human level, but also economically: The numbers in Varel are back in the black. After two years of losses, the financial year 2012 was the first profitable one. From then on, things really took off: In 2013, the house had an operating profit of over 410,000 euro; in 2014, it was 630,000 euro.

»I am pleased we will get many bookings from the local people,« says Stickdorn. »When I took over, the hotel had a really bad reputation. But now we are catering for weddings and other family events for people of the region.« Recommendations for the hotel increased from 78 percent to 95 percent, and the average occupancy rate is over 70 percent, an exceptionally good value for the industry.

»Marc Stickdorn has a very special knack for people,« Gaukler ends our conversation. »From my point of view, in Varel, he lived by example what we, at Upstalsboom, mean when we talk about mindfulness.«

Upstalsboom | A meditating director

Never did the 15 employees experience their otherwise talkative hotel director so silent. Mirco Hitzigrath moves silently and deliberately slow through the conference room; every now and then, he stops for a moment. He leads his audience through a walking meditation – a classic mindfulness exercise that psychologist Britta Hölzel also had learned in Thailand.

The idea for this joint meditation in the Upstalsboom Hotel »Meersinn« on Rügen (an island in the Baltic Sea) was born in the summer of 2014 at a breakfast meeting. As in all hotels of the Upstalsboom group, each month, six places are raffled in each of the houses for a breakfast meeting with the director and the chance to talk to him quietly for 60 minutes. »In one of those employees' breakfasts, they started talking about meditation,« the 34-year-old Hitzigrath recalls. »I told them I had already been practicing mindfulness meditation for several years. One of the employees asked if I could show them how to do that.« Immediately, everybody wanted to know more about it. »Back then, when we discussed the meditation course, my first thought was, ›more connectedness between employees and managers,‹« Service Employee Sarah Becker recalls this breakfast morning. »In addition, meditation is something unique for me. It helps me keep my cool in stressful situations.«

After a short cooling-off period, the boss agreed to a »test run.« »I informed all 70 employees about our breakfast discussion,« he says. »I sent invitations to a 30-minute employee meditation and asked for the interested parties to let me know. Shortly after, I had to send out a second email, because there was much more feedback than I expected. Fifteen interested employees could participate; the rest of the staff I had to put off for the time being.«

The topic of mindfulness was very well received. Although the hotel had belonged to the Upstalsboom group for only two years, the team quickly absorbed the company purpose and the value of mindfulness. »Since we joined Upstalsboom, we have had a significantly higher awareness of what the mission statement is all about,« says Hitzigrath. »Through this active engagement with questions of values, which is part of Upstalsboom, I sense a significantly higher affinity between the different areas of the house.«

»A hotel manager as a teacher for meditation for his employees – didn't that feel somewhat strange, initially?« I asked him. He briefly considered. »I don't think there is really a uniform image of how or what a hotel director should be. If I have the opportunity to develop my staff in any way, I like to do it, even if it means I teach them meditation.«

Once, there was another Hitzigrath, different from the one I experienced in Rügen in 2015. »I've always had a high-performance demand on me,« says the native of Hanover. »In the hotel training, I was the one with the best degree. I always wanted to achieve the best possible results.« His wife had suspected that, with his 70-hour workweek, he did not know his limits. His sister warned: »You have to take better care of yourself!« Hitzigrath recalls: »In retrospect, I did, on and off, feel those little alarm signals from my body.« However his professional success and good salary meant a lot to him.

»As a hotel director, you have responsibilities towards the management and your employees. That used to be the elixir of life for me,« he reflected self-critically. Even when an important mentor suffered a heart attack, that was still no reason to reduce the pace for Hitzigrath. He was only in his early 30s when, alongside the professional pressure, his private life started to change, and he got out of balance. Living in the professional fast lane led him into a crisis. »My father was so ill that my fiancée and I had to postpone our planned wedding,« the hotel manager remembers. »With that, something in my life, which had always been stable, started to falter.«

The impact on Hitzigrath was not long in coming: The professional high pressure forced the privately struggling perfectionist to his knees. Out of nowhere, he was overwhelmed by intense panic attacks. »You would not wish this experience on anybody,« he recalls. »When it started, I spent two days continuously in this state.« He withdrew from his daily business. For three weeks, he received intensive coaching. »Since that time, I have not only changed my behaviour, but my values, as well,« he reminiscences. Hitzigrath started with the obvious causes, such as time management. Before that, he often felt driven. Now he knows: »There is enough time. You just have to take it.« These days, he retreats regularly for a few minutes throughout the day to a quiet place to find inner stillness. With the mindfulness meditation, the realignment of his life began.

»Initially, I learned a lot from the literature on mindfulness,« he says. But Bodo Janssen, with his many retreats in the monastery, became an important inspiration for the hotel director. Like many other Upstalboomers, Janssen also invited Hitzigrath to spend a few days in the monastery. »Bodo had discussed many things about his experiences, and I could learn a lot from him,« says Hitzigrath. The daily walk and zen meditations in the monastery deepened his understanding and experience of mindfulness.

With this mindfulness practice, he not only got on top of his life again, but got his priorities straight. »Basically, I am grateful this happened,« Hitzigrath sums up. »I was able to correct the course of my life. Otherwise, I might have suffered a heart attack in maybe ten years' time.«

»You have become more attentive,« his wife noticed. »Interestingly, though, by working on myself, I developed more confidence in my environment and my employees,« says Mirco Hitzigrath. »This way, I can leave my job at work and don't carry it home as much anymore. When I spend time with my family, I am truly with them, wholeheartedly. To work 70 hours a week is not only unhealthy for me, but it also provides a bad role model for my employees.« In Mirco Hitzigrath's private life, role models and mentors have always played an important role. They greatly influenced his professional values and behaviour. »But none of my mentors ever told me I must pay attention to myself, as well,« he recalls. Today, Hitzigrath is in the position of a role model himself. »I believe we live in a time when it is essential for managers to deal with mindfulness. I am trying to live by example and pass this on to my employees.«

The test run went well. The first meditation meeting impressed the employees. »An unusual, yet familiar, situation,« says Service Employee Sandra Naujokat. »Through his quiet manner and his experience, Mr. Hitzigrath made it possible for me to relax very deeply.« The monthly meetings became weekly meetings. »This was at the request of the participants,« says the hotel director. »The thing I really like: Some people told me they now meditate at home, as well.« As a next step, many want to go to the monastery for a few days. »Again, the list of prospective participants is already jam-packed,« says Hitzigrath.

»The seminar in the monastery will mean I can get closer to inner peace,« says Service Employee Sarah Becker. »For some time now, it has been my deepest desire to learn more about it. I hope to gain a lot of positive impressions, which I can pass on to the people around me.«

Essence for Executives

Mindfulness – People finding themselves again

- People can restructure their brains and gain better access to their own potential through a different way of thinking. Mindfulness is an easy-to-learn way to get there.

- A long-term study among 5,000 people worldwide showed: Throughout 47 percent of our waking hours, our thoughts wander. However, the more participants focused on just one thing at a time, the happier they were. Regular mindfulness practice can teach this ability.
- After only eight weeks of regular mindfulness training, higher activity in the left prefrontal cortex can be measured – the part of the human brain associated with happiness and well-being. At the same time, the hippocampus (the nerve cell factory of our brains) grows.
- The American insurance company Aetna experienced, in 13,000 of its 48,000 employees, a productivity gain of $ 3,000 per person per year. This part of the workforce participated in a 12-week mindfulness course.
- Horst Inden, head of HR at the Klosterfrau sales company, stated: »Not a single participant who consistently attended our internal mindfulness courses suffered from a mental illness« (such as burn-out or depression).
- People trained in mindfulness have measurably more »insights« and, therefore, find faster solutions for problems. Heribert Gathof, CEO of Eckes-Granini Germany, reports: »Ideas emerge in such clarity that I did not have before.«

An epilogue in keywords – What you could do now

- At your workplace, look for like-minded people with whom you can create common internal pictures of the direction in which you want to develop together. From chapter 1, you know: »Executives who have successfully created a human-centred and economically thriving culture started by developing strong internal pictures of the future state of their company.«
- In the beginning, focus on the implementation of the contents of two to three chapters. »Less is more« is an old truism, which in many companies, becomes true time after time. Most likely, you have too many projects to deal with, anyway.
- Get feedback before you start! For example, if you think »meaningfulness« is already lived in your company, ask your workforce about it. The same applies to the key learnings of the remaining chapters. Two-thirds of the executives I worked with were initially wrong in their opinion of how their employees feel. Don't start any changes, based entirely on your assumptions.
- Involve your employees and your organisation in the change. Remember chapter 3: Employees want to participate; this gives their work much higher meaning. To change something, imagine your business environment to be an Ikea box: Let people assemble the box!
- Give this book to people with whom you work closely. If you want to change something in your work environment. Successful change is easier when initiated together.

If you have further questions how to implement these learnings in your organisation, just email spp@sebastian-purps-pardigol.com.

Acknowledgements

I would like to give thanks to some people. Some of you won't even know how important your part was in this book coming into being.

First, I want to thank my son, Paul, who was born two months before completing the manuscript. I had reasonable doubt whether I would find enough strength and peace to send the book to my publisher on time. Paul loves to sleep for many hours at a time – either in his bed or in the arms of his parents. Thus my fears quickly faded. I had only to shift my writing to other times of the day which, initially, were unfamiliar. Now, I am happy to have finished the manuscript and to spend more time with him. He has recently started with the social smile and has already wrapped us around his finger.

A significant credit for the deep relaxation of Paul and the fact that, despite everything else going on, I could keep writing, goes to my wife, Ines, whom I thank with all my heart. »Last night I dreamed about your book,« she said one morning. That was the moment I realised how »all consuming« this project was, even for her.

A very important role in ensuring this book would come into being in this context goes to Jörg-Achim Zoll and Andrea Rehmsmeier. It was Jörg-Achim who, during a long walk through the forest, tactfully suggested I throw the already-authored chapters overboard and write the book in an entirely different way. He wrapped it all up so courteously that I, ultimately, got the impression this had been my decision all along. All my thanks go out to him, because by now, I can see it in black and white: The book has become so much better for it! Andrea, meanwhile, tirelessly tried to convey grammatical discipline to me. After I had my way with the historical present tense, the past perfect tense, and all the other tenses (I did not even know), she always swept the mess together and gave my chapters grammatical consistency, »so you are not losing your readers.« Thank you, Andrea!

Jennifer Deventer was the woman in the background. She spent a lot of time following up on my vague search indications, which usually went something like this: »There was this study I once read about ... It went something like that ...« She always found what I was looking for so desperately. Thank you, Jenny.

It was Nils Cornelissen who introduced me to Jenny. But not only this, he represents a special blend of intellectual sharpness and benevolence – something I am often grateful for. To have him as a sparring partner and friend (in particular, for the final decision on the title of this book) was a great addition.

At a very early stage, Sabine Jung played an important role in developing this book, and time after time, sent me brilliant title suggestions. Although we used none for this book, I have enough titles now for the next five books. Dearest Sabine, thank you for that.

I want to thank Nicola Fritze who, over the years, gave me direction in my professional development, simply by the way she saw me and that she could express her point of view credibly. This was helpful in many key decisions.

Silvia Kaufhold was an important sparring partner for me. Throughout the early important phases of my life, I was inspired by her professional attitude, something I am forever grateful for.

I also want to thank Campus Verlag and, especially, my editor, Stephanie Walter. Having me as an author was certainly not easy at times. Sometimes, she had to mediate between her colleagues and me.

I would like to thank an important companion, who inspired me through our discussions, to get going with this book. Just as any good friend would do – if I complained that all this took more my time – he rewarded me with courage through his personal experience. Dear Gerald, thank you for your trust over the recent years; I could learn from you to take things a little bit slower.

Commented Sources

To prepare for this book, I accessed 450 articles and studies. Some were helpful simply to know about. In others, I would find one decisive sentence, which would help me continue. And about 120 documents contained much substance; these I have already partly addressed in this book. I would like to recommend texts which deserve a closer look.

1. »Plasticity in the Frequency Representation of Primary Auditory Cortex Following Discrimination Training in Adult Owl Monkeys«, G. H. Recanzone, C. E. Schreiner, and M. M. Merzenich, *The Journal of Neuroscience*, January 1993.

Do you remember the experiment from chapter 1? When I asked you to imagine putting on a headset and listening to a sequence of strange sounds? At the same time, I asked you to imagine I was tapping on your hand with my pen. Depending on what you focused on, one could detect a change in either one's cerebral cortex, which processes auditory stimuli, or the part of one's brain responsible for processing the sensations of one's hands. The key finding: Our attention determines whether and where neuroplasticity occurs. If you want to read more studies on this topic, the following are recommended: »Functional Reorganization of Primary Somatosensory Cortex in Adult Owl Monkeys After Behaviorally Controlled Tactile stimulation«, William M. Jenkins, Michael M. Merzenich, Marlene T. Ochs, Terry Allard and Eliana Guk-Robles, *Journal of Neurophysiology*, Volume 63, January 1990. Also: »Cortical Plasticity and Memory«, Michael M. Merzenich and Koichi Sameshima, *Current Opinion in Neurobiology*, 1993, 3: 187–196.

2. »Effects of Social Exclusion on Cognitive Processes: Anticipated Aloneness Reduces Intelligent Thought«, Roy F. Baumeister, Jean M. Twenge, Christopher K. Nuss, *Journal of Personality and Social Psychology*, Volume 83, 2002. Hopefully, I have conveyed to you the importance of connectedness and belonging to people. Roy Baumeister was the man who made the participants of his study believe their future would be without friends and would be filled with failed relationships. In the ensuing intelligence test, those manipulated subjects' test results were 27 percent below those of a control group.

I like Baumeister's study very much, because it is intuitive and easy to understand. The idea of experiencing a lonely future led to an uneasy feeling in many of my workshop participants. The memory of the fear of social isolation is not affected … but best read in Baumeister.

3. »Job Control, Personal Characteristics, and Heart Disease«, Hans Bosma, Stephen A. Stansfeld, and Michael G. Marmot, *Journal of Occupational Health Psychology*, Volume 3, 1998

Some of the most exciting long-term studies of the past century include Whitehall 1 and Whitehall 2, in which 18,000 and 10,000 government employees respectively were investigated. The raw material of these studies is extensive and publicly available for scientific purposes. There are numerous reports about the raw data. I especially liked the one by Hans Bosma, in which he elaborates about the finding that more self-efficacy leads to a lower risk of heart disease.

4. »Can Personality Be Changed? The Role of Beliefs in Personality and Change«, Carol S. Dweck, *Current Directions in Psychological Science*, Volume 17, of 2008.

Unfortunately, because of stringency, I could not bring Carol Dweck into the book. Sometimes, less is more. Nevertheless, I like her article very much, because it makes the influence of the internal pictures (beliefs) traceable to the performance of test subjects. Dweck has released another wonderful article, which elaborates on the subject of how children should be praised, so they can optimally develop: »Praise for Intelligence Can Undermine Children's Motivation and Performance«, Claudia M. Mueller and Carol S. Dweck, *Journal of Personality and Social Psychology*, Volume 75., 1998

5. »Experience-Induced Neurogenesis in the Senescent Dentate Gyrus«, Gerd Kempermann, H. Georg Kuhn, and Fred Gage, *The Journal of Neuroscience*, May 1, 1998

Fred Gage is a neuroscientist, who was invited to annual meetings with the Dalai Lama in Dharamsala. He is also a descendant of Phineas Gage who, in 1848, in an accident, got an iron bar shot through his prefrontal cortex. Fred Gage has been a key figure in the study of neurogenesis, the formation of new brain cells. Basically, his study says: The more experience we get, the faster our brains will grow. If you want to know more about this, get his study. Matching the content, also look at this study, even if it has been quoted countless times before. »Navigation-related Structural Change in the hippocampi of taxi drivers«, Eleanor A. Maguire, David G. Gadian, Ingrid S. Johnsrude, Catriona D. Good, John Ashburner, Richard S.J. Frackowiak, and Christopher D. Frith, *Proceedings of the National Academy of Sciences*, Volume 97, 2000. This is the famous taxi driver study from London, which examined the hippocampi of people in this profession: Taxi drivers in England's capital must memorise thousands of roads and dozens of attractions. This extraordinary demand causes neuroplastic change. This study is very catchy and worth reading.

6. »Seasonal Recruitment of Hippocampal Neurons in Adult Free-ranging Black-capped Chickadees«, Anat Barnea and Fernando Nottebohm, Proc. Natl. Acad. Sci. USA, Vol 91, pp. 11217–11221, November 1994 Neurobiology

I would like to report about a study my friend Gerald Hüther often mentions. It is about South American domestic and wild donkeys. They are genetically identical, but neuronally different. Wild donkeys have a thicker neocortex because, through all those challenging experiences of living in the wild, they form more neural networks. However, there was a better study with black-capped chickadees, which shows something similar: Domestic chickadees show less neuroplastic change in their brains than their wild counterparts, because the latter must master complex challenges. This study proves: Our experiences shape the neural structures in our heads.

7. »Relationship of Parental Bonding Styles with Grey Matter Volume of dorsolateral prefrontal cortex in Young Adults«, Kosuke Narita, Yuichi Takei, Masashi Suda, Yoshiyuki Aoyama, Toru Uehara, Hirotaka Kosaka, Makoto Amanuma, Masato Fukuda, Masahiko Mikuni, *Progress in Neuro-Psychopharmacology and Biological Psychiatry*, Volume 34, Issue 4.

In this study, a team led by Kosuke Narita examined the neuroplastic effects of neglect and overprotection. Fifty Japanese subjects underwent brain scans while in their 20s. This was accompanied by an in-depth study on how the participants experienced their upbringing. Both groups of people – those who lacked experiences because of neglect and those who were overly protected from »all dangers« – showed changes in their brains. There was a measurable decrease in important areas of the prefrontal cortex.

8. »Man's search for meaning: The case of Legos«, Dan Ariely, Emir Kamenica, Drazen Prelec, *Journal of Economic Behavior & Organization* 67 (2008) 671–677.

Ariely's experiment is by name special, because it adapts the title of Viktor Frankl's book, *Man's Search for Meaning* – a book well worth reading if you are interested in the meaning of life. Frankl was the founder of logotherapy or meaning-centred psychotherapy.

Ariely is one of the most remarkable scientists who have ever crossed my path. Should you ever see a video of him and wonder why his face looks strange: He had a serious accident in which a large part of the skin of his body burned. Ariely tells the whole story and describes the very painful healing process in this written document: http://people.duke.edu/~dandan/webfiles/mypain.pdf.

Back to his experiment, which I have described extensively in chapter 6. He beautifully demonstrated the importance of valuing and respecting work results. In many organisations, I experienced this is missing. It is one of the most frequently mentioned points in employee surveys. I just returned from a multi-day workshop, where the participants confirmed this to their bosses: »We lack appreciation!« Ariely's small, yet wonderful, experiment shows us what happens when employees experience appreciation: Motivation increases by a factor of three!

9. »Fluid Intelligence and Brain Functional Organization in Aging Yoga and Meditation Practitioners«, Tim Gard, Maxime Taquet, Rohan Dixit, Britta K. Hölzel, Yves-Alexandre de Montjoye, Narayan Brach, David H. Salat, Bradford C. Dickerson, Jeremy R. Gray and Sara W. Lazar. *Frontiers in Aging Neuroscience*, April 2014, Volume 6, Article 76.

Sara Lazar and Britta Hölzel, who both participated in the study, belong to a group of scientists from the Harvard Medical School, Boston, who in previous years, published several studies in which, with the help of brain scans, they demonstrated a functional and structural change in the brains of meditating people. This article delves into a direction that could, ultimately, show meditation has a positive impact on the age-related decrease of cognitive functions. Although the scientists are still at the very beginning, the initial results are encouraging. Fluid intelligence – the ability to think logically and solve problems – decreases with age. In this study, the researchers compared the cognitive abilities of 47 people. A special focus was on their ability to maintain attention. Some of the interviewed people had been yoga and meditation practitioners for several years. The results show fluid intelligence was lower in older, compared to younger, participants. However, there was a significant difference in the older group: While the fluid intelligence – and the cognitive functions – of the control group (aged 40 to 70 years) decreased by almost 50 percent, in yogis and meditating participants, it decreased by just 20 percent.

Index